MW00627771

THE
LADDER
UP

SECRET STEPS
TO JEWISH HAPPINESS

BY R. L. KREMNIZER

בס"ד

THE LADDER UP

Secret Steps
To Jewish Happiness

By R.L. Kremnizer

Sichos In English
788 Eastern Parkway
Brooklyn, New York 11213

הי' תהא שנת נפלאות דגולות

THE LADDER UP
Secret Steps to Jewish Happiness

Published and Copyrighted © by
Sichos In English
788 Eastern Parkway • Brooklyn, New York 11213
Tel. (718) 778-5436

ISBN 1-8814-0010-7

5754 • 1994

Printed by Books-Etc in Bulgaria.

DEDICATION

This book is dedicated to
the Lubavitcher Rebbe
Rabbi Menachem M. Schneerson
who (see list p. 116)
throughout this volume
is referred to simply as
"the Rebbe".

ACKNOWLEDGMENTS

I owe a debt of gratitude to all the many teachers and people who have made this book possible who are too numerous to mention individually.

Some however must be mentioned by name:

Rabbi Feldman with Rabbi Lesches and the Sydney Yeshiva Centre for providing constantly refertilized ground.

My first teacher Rabbi M. Kantor who showed me the possibility of seeing in color for the first time.

Rabbi A. Perlow and Rabbi M. Gourarie for helping to structure all the *shiurim* and Rabbi Gourarie for then adding all the footnotes, checking the material and being supportively critical.

M. Moss, the best *chavrusa* a man could have.

Pesach Johns whose recordings of my weekly *shiur* made much of the material efficiently reaccessible.

Velvel Steinberg for the idea of the book.

Most of all to my dear wife, Ann, for her encouragement, support, proof reading and correcting, all with unshakable patience and good humor.

RLK

CONTENTS

PART THREE

SECRETS OF THE FESTIVALS CHAPTER:

PART THREE

EPILOGUE

PART ONE
BUILDING BLOCKS

2 **The Ladder Up**

READ THIS FIRST

As we go, it will become common ground that Moshe received the Torah on Mount Sinai, comprising 613 *mitzvos* (commands) which were to be carried out by 600,000-odd male souls who, together with their wives and children, amounted to three million people.[1] These souls (or their fragments) have been coming back through various *gilgulim* (cycles) ever since, in order to complete those 613 *mitzvos*.[2] Great secrets of Torah were also received by Moshe and communicated to certain select Jews in each generation since then.

Until the time prior to the dawn of the Industrial Revolution, it was forbidden for Jews to learn the secret side of Torah unless they understood the whole of the Talmud, were over forty and married.[3] These three conditions exempted most ordinary people from access to those secrets.

Many secrets of Torah are embodied in a volume known as "The *Zohar*" which contains these traditions as written down by R. Shimon Bar Yochai.

The teachings of this book were withheld for a thousand years with a prophecy that at a time when required it would be revealed. That time corresponds exactly to the Industrial Revolution[4]. At the same time as the process of technology began, there set in a deepening darkness in the world in terms of obvious spirituality. Clearly, it is easier to see G-d in the mountains than in a city street. So in order to shed light into the spiritual gloom the secret side of the Torah was to be released.

---

1.   See *Makkos* 23b.
2.   See *Tanya, Iggeres HaKodesh* Epistle 7.
3.   See *Rambam, Hilchos Yesodei HaTorah* 2:12.
4.   See lengthy explanation in *Likkutei Sichos*, Vol. 15, p 42ff (Noach 2).

The teachings of the *Zohar* were refined and restructured into the form of *Chassidus,* first with the Baal Shem Tov, then the Mezritcher Maggid and then through an inner circle of *Rebbeim* throughout Europe. These secrets have been whispered and then articulated more and more loudly by the Rebbes of Lubavitch *(Chabad).* (See notes at end).

From the time that information began being released, and for the first time in Jewish history, an ordinary Jew had access to properly understand the greatest principles in the universe. We will deal with some of these as building blocks. When concepts are on board, we will apply them to specifics and then to the world. With this information a Jew can soar into the heavens.

BUILDING BLOCK NO. 1

HASHGOCHA PROTIS
(DIVINE PROVIDENCE)

Hashgochah Protis (Divine Providence) is probably one of the most misunderstood concepts in Jewish thinking. It is so misunderstood being confused with notions of fatalism and lack of free choice. Properly appreciating this principle is so important that it must become a point of focus in every Jew's life. The more one is attuned to it, the easier one's life can be; the less one understands it, the more random, the more complicated and the more confusing life is.

We begin with a *moshul* (example):

Picture the Mona Lisa; a lady with her hands folded, a smile on her face, mountains in the background and a winding road. By concentrating hard, we can build up as accurate a picture of the Mona Lisa as our memory permits. But that mind-picture depends for its existence on our concentration. If our concentration is broken, the picture disappears. If we sit concentrating intently on the Mona Lisa and the phone rings with someone important on the line, our concentration will break and the Mona Lisa will be gone.

The Baal Shem Tov publicized a concept based on a verse in *Tehillim* (Psalms) not previously generally well known[5]. The effect of this explanation was to show that *Hashem* (G-d) did not create the world and move away from it (in the sense that, say, a television once made then has an independent life).

The process of creating is continuous and is maintained all the time. If it were to stop, even for an instant, the world would revert to nothingness. This is an absolutely fundamental first principle. Everything physical depends for its existence on being recreated

---

5.   See *Tanya, Shaar HaYichud VehaEmunah* Chapter 1.

every moment and all the time. From continents and oceans to microbes on pin heads; clouds and wind to the number of hairs on our heads and the direction they point. If the recreating process were to stop for a moment the world would disappear in the same way the painting would disappear the moment concentration ceased.

Why is this such an important principle? Because there is an erroneous consensus of opinion even amongst people who believe in G-d that He in some way established an evolving machine which runs, and because He is a Great Engineer, no repair is necessary. Some even maintain that the machine runs randomly. So the first principle of Divine Providence is that the process of creation is continuous: it requires *Hashem's* effortless concentration, as it were, every split second to continue to bring physicality into existence.

The Baal Shem Tov further extended the concept of *Hashgochah Protis* to explain that *Hashem* controls everything every split second as it is being brought into existence. A leaf on the ground being nudged by a breath of wind is not by accident but has a specific reason and also relates to the general intent and purpose of creation. (Later we will discuss the one area *Hashem* has delegated namely human free choice. We will learn that this free choice is restricted to the area of moral decisions.)

There is a story about two great Rebbes; Reb Zusha of Anapole and his brother, Reb Elimelech of Lizansk. The two brothers decided they would renounce whatever worldly connections they had and undertake a spiritual journey by traveling from place to place in poverty. They came to an inn and, having no money, they prevailed upon the Jewish owner to allow them to stay, sleeping in front of the fire in the main room.

While they slept and in the early hours of the morning, a group of Cossacks opened the inn ordering the owner to bring vodka. They began to sing and then dance and, as they danced, noticed hapless Reb Zusha who was lying closer into the room than Reb Elimelech in the shadows. In delight the Cossacks began to kick Reb Zusha as they danced taking it in turn to enjoy the sport. Between dances, while the Cossacks were refilling their vodka, Reb Elimelech suggested to change positions with his brother so he could take a turn and give his brother rest. Reluctantly Reb Zusha agreed and they changed places.

The Cossacks began to dance again but spied two Jews! In a spirit of justice they resolved to leave alone the first victim and instead kick the "other" Jew. This is *Hashgochah Protis*. It was Reb Zusha's turn to be kicked. He can move. He can move nearer the fire or further away from the fire. He can change places. No good. If he is to be kicked he will be kicked. The only question is why is he being kicked.

A second fundamental principle is that *Hashem* is all good and that therefore there can be no bad at all.[6] Everything that happens in physical creation has to be ultimately for the good.[7] This is a difficult principle which will be much explained later. For the present, it should be understood that things can only be *apparently* not good. It then follows that when one finds oneself in an environment, whether that environment is physical or emotional or spiritual, and if one understands the concept of *Hashgochah Protis*, the notion that *Hashem* controls everything in creation, then the shuddering fact is that one is in that environment, *deliberately*.

What then about free choice?

It is a tenet of most civilized people's belief that we have free choice. This too is a misunderstood concept. We only have free choice in relation to moral decisions.[8] That means that a Jew has free choice in relation to 613 *mitzvos,* 248 positive *mitzvos* and 365 negative *mitzvos*.[9] He has no free choice on which direction he chooses to drive to work (providing there is no moral decision involved).

A gentile has a free choice only in seven areas; those areas of the seven *mitzvos* of Noah[10]. Admittedly, those seven areas amount to

---

6.   See *Midrash Rabbah Bereishis* Chapter 51; *Iggeres HaKodesh* Epistle 11.
7.   See *Tanya,* Chapter 26.
8.   See *Berachos* 33b. "Everything is in the hands of Heaven except for fear of Heaven".
9.   See *Likkutei Torah, Emor* 38b.
10.   See *Sefer HaMaamarim Basi LeGani,* p. 53.

very many strands in the fabric of life. Nevertheless, in every other area, he is part of the process of *Hashgochah Protis*. In every area other than the 613 *mitzvos*, a Jew is also part of the process of *Hashgochah Protis*.

These are very different notions to those of fatalism. Fatalists imagine what will be will be. This is wrong. We believe the ongoing creative process happening around us is *directly influenced* by the moral decisions man makes by exercising his free choice. So, when *Am Yisrael* (the Jewish people) are living properly, the environment is influenced positively.

When *Am Yisrael* fails, then the environment suffers. More of this later.

So when a Jew understands this cardinal principle that his environment is totally and absolutely controlled and yet that control by *Hashem* is influenced by his moral decisions, he understands that he has been positioned there deliberately.

Why?

This question needs answering unless one is going to spend his life bumping into doors the way as do, unfortunately, many Jews today.

BUILDING BLOCK NO. 2

YERIDAH (DESCENT)
FOR *ALIYAH* (ASCENT)

Every Jewish *neshomah* (soul) in its *gilgul* (life cycle) in a particular body has descended in order to afford it the *opportunity* to do certain specific *mitzvos* and thus realize its potential. Its *yeridah* (decent) is for the sole purpose of a subsequent *aliyah* (ascent)[11] and, as we will see, as everything physical is a reflection of its spiritual counterpart, so it is with everything. Every descent is for the purpose of an ascent. Indeed, there is no ascent without a *prior* descent. This is true of souls, of nations and of each individual in his own life.[12]

This is staggering information. Apply it to a position one dislikes: for example, a traffic jam. There are two ways to approach a traffic jam; to be outraged at being helplessly trapped, or to try to understand what is going on and determine the reason for being in that traffic jam.

Suppose some incompetent, insensitive driver drives out on the wrong side, oblivious to traffic, causing an accident. The immediate emotional response of most people is rage. Know however that it is possible to avoid frustration. Know that it is possible to avoid anger. How? By really *understanding Hashgochah Protis*. Understanding that being in a specific position at a specific moment (not the result of a moral decision) is deliberate. And if being placed there is for the good[13], and only for the good, there can be no anger. There can only be an appreciation of the need for growth, the need for an *aliyah* from the *yeridah*.

---

11.   See *Torah Or, Bereishis* p. 30a.
12.   See *expression in the verse Koheles* 2:13, *Yisron Ho'or Mitoch Hachoshech*. See also *Likkutei Sichos*, Vol. 20, p. 528.
13.   See *Makkos 23a and the explanation in Likkutei Sichos*, Vol. 19, p. 67.

There can be no worry.

There can be no fear.

If one's environment is totally controlled and deliberate and for the good, what place is there for worry? Or fear? Or anger?

This is a great level to attain? This requires practice and effort? Agreed.

But what these secrets in Torah promise is a light clearer than any previously revealed in the world. To see the best view, it is a hard climb.

The Alter Rebbe[14], the founder of the *Chabad* movement, in his book, *"Tanya"*, the cornerstone of *Chassidus*, quotes the verse that says that it is within the grasp of every Jew to be able to do.[15] It requires training. But it is within reach of every Jew. Imagine a private world where there is no fear and no anger and no worry. This is the position to which a Jew can climb. Why? Because he understands that his immediate position is absolutely deliberately orchestrated by *Hashem,* being recreated for him at that moment in time.

Any apparent negative happening therefore is only for the purpose of growth.

What then if this position appears bad like the traffic jam? Or the lunatic driver?

There are three *berachos* (blessings). *Bonim* (children), *chai* (health) and *parnossah* (money, sustenance). They are the three *berachos* which Jews receive. It is rare to be allowed all three. More common is for a Jew to receive two or sometimes one. (This will be discussed in detail later). But what happens when a person, used to receiving one of these *berachos*, is suddenly denied? A Jew loses money or his child sickens or, even worse, G-d Forbid, dies.

So why is that happening?

In the last three hundred years the ordinary Jew who learns *Chassidus* has become privy to this unbelievable secret. The secret

---

14. See notes on *Lubavitcher Rebbes* at end of the book.
15. See *Deuteronomy* 3:14.

bears repeating: Every descent in physical creation is *necessary* for the purpose of an ascent to a point higher than before the descent. The rule is not an ascent and then a descent. The rule is that *in order* to achieve an ascent, first there must be a descent. This is a stunning revelation. It is a revelation so great as to change one's appreciation of the world forever. There is no bad in the world. There cannot be any bad in the world. There is that which we *perceive* as being bad. Why do we perceive it as being bad? Because we see it as being unsuitable for our position as it is revealed to us at a given point in time.

The Rebbe has a famous letter[16] where he replies to somebody that a Martian entering an operating theatre would not imagine that the surgeon and his team, cutting the patient open, were doing something intended for the ultimate good of the patient. But, in fact, what is happening in that operating theatre is that, leaving aside personal gratification, that medical team is dedicated to doing something positive for that person being interfered with.

In life the descent is usually obvious; but perceiving the ultimate ascent?. That is a whole lifetime's effort, but we will learn its structure together.

Often a person will be compelled to find the path to his ascent. For example, assume it was for his good for a multi-millionaire living in Sydney, Australia, to move to *Eretz Yisrael.* A computer programmer, given the job of moving this man to *Eretz Yisrael,* will have a difficult task. The subject has everything he wants where he is. His wife and family are there. His matching BMW's in the garage are there. His holiday house in the ski country is there. He is not moving to *Eretz Yisrael.* But, take away his money; bankrupt him; is there a better chance now?

Now assume that for that person it is an ascent to go to *Eretz Yisrael.* When he loses all his money, he views his position as disastrous (the descent). When he reaches *Eretz Yisrael* and finds a new life and new happiness, he may understand that without the

---

16. Reprinted in *A Thought For the Week,* Vol. IV, p. 99.

descent which was for the purpose of the ascent there could have been no ascent.

A person can regard the descent critically, blame G-d, blame the system and beat his head against a wall. Become angry or worried or frightened. Alternatively, he can try to understand what is going on with his life and try to see where he is going. Sometimes he may need to access a Rebbe. But, invariably, there is an opportunity, where there is descent, to recognize the opportunity for an ascent. We will learn how together.

BUILDING BLOCK NO. 3

CHOCHMAH, BINAH & *DAAS*
(DO YOU STILL SMOKE?)
THE GRID OF *CHABAD*

Let us pretend there is an imaginary doctor living in the sixties. He smokes a couple of packs of cigarettes a day and has an unimportant chronic cough, but is otherwise relatively normal.

One day he notices that every patient for whom he prescribes cough antidotes, smokes. He has a sudden flash; maybe smoking and coughing are related. Second flash; maybe smoking is bad for the health generally!

The flashes are known in *Chassidus* as *chochmah*. The flash has no length or breadth — it is a flash point of momentary and potent light.

Now, suppose he begins to do some investigating. He begins to study cases of chest related disorders and gathers statistics. Slowly, a pattern in those numbers begins to emerge. There is a definite correlation between the smoking population and the chest related disorder population.

This is *binah*. The process of investigating and understanding the implications of that first flash. Examining the length and breadth of information to build up a reasoned logical proposition formed by a thorough understanding of the concept.

A conclusion is reached; smoking is bad for health. Indeed when the *binah* process is finally complete, a proposition is born from the *chochmah* and then the *binah*. The proposition can be formulated like this:[17]

---

17.   For all of the above see *Tanya*, Chapter 3

SMOKING KILLS YOU

Now, here comes the jackpot question, does our doctor give up smoking? And the incredible answer? Not necessarily. Our imaginary doctor knows smoking will kill him and yet he does not necessarily give it up. Why? He has no *daas* in smoking. *daas* is the level of taking on board information arrived through *chochmah* and then *binah*, so that a permanent change is effected[18]. No one in their right mind can smoke. The reason they do is they have no *daas* in relation to this *chochmah* and *binah*.

Small children have no *daas*. This is the reason they will do things entirely contrary to even their own logic let alone that of the parent. It is a waste of time to take a four year old child and reason with him as to why he should keep away from a swimming pool.

Even in the unlikely event the child can accept the *chochmah* or hear examples of tragedies which become the *binah*, the child has no *daas*, and is in critical danger near the water if it cannot swim.

So then, all are levels of understanding. The flash is understanding, so is the statistical research, as is the change of behavior. We learn in *Chassidus* however, that each separate category of *chochmah*, *binah* and *daas* are necessary. However, it is impossible to be spiritually mature and upwardly mobile without the *daas*.

A Jewish thief prays to G-d for success. Consider that. He prays because he is a Jew. Jews do deals with G-d. If G-d lets me do this, I will do that in return. Help my child with this problem and I will donate a computer to such and such an institution. But how can a thief pray for success? He knows (*chochmah*) there is a G-d He knows (*binah*) that he cannot profit by going against His will. How can a man possibly profit from behaving contrary to *Hashem's* will?

Our Jewish thief steals because he is a spiritual child. He has no *daas* in relation to stealing. This may be for many varied reasons, all of which came from his *yetzer hora* (evil inclination) (see Building

---

18.   See *Sefer HaMaamarim* 5670, p. 112ff; *Torah Or, Mishpotim* p. 148.

Block No. 6) but the conclusion is the same; in relation to this *mitzvah* at least, he has no *daas*.

In a spiritually mature person, intellect rules emotion. Intellect is *chochmah*, *binah* and *daas*. In order to complete an intellectual grasp of any matter, all three ingredients must be there.

What we learn together here will introduce the *chochmah* and *binah* of how to live a purposeful and therefore happy life. For better or for worse, honesty requires that it be known that the *daas* must come from the reader.

BUILDING BLOCK NO. 4

SELF ESTEEM & ARROGANCE
HUMILITY & INFERIORITY

The Second *Bais HaMikdash* (the Second Temple) was destroyed through causeless hatred of one Jew to another[19] and the Rebbe tells us the only way it will be rebuilt is through causeless love.[20] In our generation, the *mitzvah* of *ahavas Yisrael* (love of a fellow Jew) is critically important. It is impossible to understand the dynamics of this *mitzvah* without understanding some aspects of the Jewish psyche and the Jewish *neshomah*. To do this, we must first understand two basic opposites in Jewish personality.

Everything in creation has a positive side and a negative side. Jews have a *Nefesh HaBahamis* (an animal soul) and a *Nefesh HoElokis* (a G-dly soul).[21] This is dealt with in detail elsewhere in this book. There is light and dark. There is *kedushah* (holiness) and there is *kelipah* (the absence of holiness).

In the human psyche, a person has a positive and negative side. The negative side of self-importance is *yeshus* (conceit, arrogance). *Yeshus* connotes boasting, feelings of exaggerated self-importance, perverse feelings of superiority and the like. *Yeshus* is *kelipah*.

The positive side of self-importance is self-esteem which connotes security in one's own position, a real understanding of one's abilities and one's gifts from *Hashem*. True self-esteem is consistent with *kedushah*[22].

At the other end of the spectrum is a person's sense of his lack of self-importance. This too has a light and dark, a positive and a

---

19. See *Yoma* 9b.
20. See for example *Likkutei Sichos*, Vol. 13 p. 292.
21. See *Tanya*, Chapters 1 & 2.
22. See *HaYom Yom*, Entry 26 Cheshvan.

negative. The negative is feelings of inferiority and therefore depression[23]. This results in an ability to only see the bad and produces anxiety and forebodings of ill and of evil.

The positive side of lack of self-importance is *bittul* (humility) which connotes self-nullification; A healthy perception of one's self, one's *yeshus*, as unimportant.

The dynamics of the above distinctions are much misunderstood in contemporary society. Psychiatrists and marriage counselors flounder because of a lack of understanding of what we will learn together. Frequently, therapists advise clients to overcome their depression-related problems (a negative) by growing their *yeshus*, which is an equal negative. The goal should be to replace the negative with a positive. Replace their *yeshus* with *bittul*. Change, with training, the selfish for the selfless. Interestingly, selflessness is consistent with self-esteem, and confidence. Selfishness is consistent with anxiety and depression.

To understand this, we need to discuss the notion in Torah of space. Feelings of *yeshus* are directly related to space. There is a story of the *Chosid* who complained to his Rebbe that everyone in his shul was always treading on his toes. The Rebbe's reply was to caution him on the size of his feet[24].

If too much space is required, there is a result of being pinched.

How much space is one allowed? What is an appropriate amount of space? If too much space risks pinching, how much is too much space, how much is too little space?

The Rebbe Rashab[25] explains[26] that causeless hatred, mentioned before, is a result of this question of space. Everyone has experienced a newcomer into a meeting or social gathering previously interrelating comfortably. Upon his arrival, New Face takes over and does all the talking. He takes up too much room. Those present, robbed of their fair amount of space, resent New

---

23. See *Tanya*, Chapter 26.
24. See *Sefer HaMaamarim Melukot* Vol. 6, p. 38.
25. See notes on *Lubavitcher Rebbes* at end of the book.
26. For the following explanation see *Kuntres Heichaltzu (Sefer HaMaamarim* 5659, p. 53) Chapter 3 onwards. (See also *HaYom Yom*, Entry 10 Teves).

Face and the theft of their space. Dislike, even hatred, of New Face is born. Only later is it accorded reasons.

He is too fat; too gregarious; bad mannered; untidy — whatever subjective reason each person is prepared to attribute to him. The more sophisticated a person is, the more sophisticated the reasons. But all of this is really a rationalization of the fact that New Face is committing larceny of his neighbors' intellectual and emotional domains.

We accord each other different spaces in different times and places. For example, a lecturer, speaking to his audience, has the space to talk by common agreement, by consensus. But if he were to visit, for example, a dentist and sought the same space in the waiting room he took up in the lecture, people would correctly feel outraged. He may be entitled to that quantity of space in the lecture by common consent, but it is not the space to which he is entitled in the waiting room.

This concept of space is so important that it requires further embellishment. Sometimes, when people abdicate space by consent, they are jealous of the recipient's undisturbed right to it. For example, at a concert, space is delegated to the musicians. If a member of the audience eats his chips too loudly or rolls his Jaffa's down the aisle, people become upset. Why? Because this person is stealing the space delegated to the musicians.

The robbing of one another's spaces is the fundamental root cause of all hatred. For this reason, it is critical to understand spaces correctly.

Back to *yeshus* and *bittul*. Self-esteem and being certain about being correct bears no relation to arrogance, boasting and false feelings of self-importance as we have said. It is a recognition of a fact. For example, if a person is seven foot six tall, he must recognize that he is taller than other people. He cannot describe himself even to himself as medium or average. He recognizes his height and he recognizes it as being beyond his *control*. It has to do with the partnership of his father, his mother and G-d. There is a genetic biological reason perhaps influenced by environment. But clearly that reason is outside of his control. To boast about being seven foot six tall would therefore be stupid. Equally, there can be no false modesty about the fact. There is no investiture in being seven foot six tall of the person's *effort*. There is a simple recognition of a fact of seven foot six tall.

If one person has a G-d-given ability to play tennis, it is idiotic of him to imagine that he is in some way superior to somebody who has no ability to play tennis. The next person has different givens. A person who has certainty about his own gifts need have no false modesty about them nor a sense of importance because of them.

Moses, of whom the Torah says was the most humble man who ever lived, was certain of his credentials. Why? Because he knew his spiritual height[27].

The terror of a *Tzaddik* (perfectly righteous man) is whether he is living out his potential as a *Tzaddik* properly. The question becomes — is being seven foot six being *utilized* fully? It would be more logical for a seven foot six person to realize his potential and play basketball than to pretend that he is really three foot two and seek to be a midget in a circus. His mandate is to live out his potential with his G-d-given gifts.

Moses recognized his gifts. His humility came from the all-consuming concern of whether those recognized gifts were being fully utilized in serving *Hashem*. This is the question of the humble. The greater the humility, the greater the terror of the question.

Conversely, a man may be, and know, he is five foot two and seek to convince others and himself that he is seven foot six. He knows he is only five foot two. Not only that, but he believes being seven foot six is a personal achievement. He tries to be unaware that he is five foot two and that it has nothing to do with his achievement. His job is to take his genetic fact and to make the best of being five foot two. There is no chance of him making the best of being seven foot six. This is not required of him. To make the best of being four foot two is equally absurd because his opportunities commence with being five foot two.

---

27.   See for example *Likkutei Sichos*, Vol. 13, p. 30ff.

The story is told of a Rebbe and *shamus* (assistant) who were to be the guests of a town in Poland known to have contained many great scholars. Aware that this Rebbe was very learned, they prepared questions for him to answer. It happened that as they approached the town, the Rebbe noticed the *shamus* downcast. Upon inquiry, the *shamus* admitted to being jealous of the honor and compliments paid to his Rebbe. The Rebbe replied that after all he was the Rebbe and the *shamus* the *shamus*. [I am seven foot six, you are five foot two. Enjoy being five foot two and let me be — and have the problems of being — seven foot six.] Nevertheless, the *shamus* requested of the Rebbe to change clothes. He begged to be the Rebbe, just once, and the Rebbe to be the *shamus*. The Rebbe agreed. They changed clothes and, upon entry to the town, they were confronted with a welcoming committee. After normal formalities, it finally came time for learned questions. The most respected of the congregation cleared his throat and asked the *shamus* an extremely difficult question drawing on many aspects of Torah and Talmud. The *shamus* was of course devastated and listened with his mouth half open. Finally, he squeaked, "That's a question? That is so easy a question, I will put it to my *shamus*...".

Back to space.

People will clearly recognize that a man is seven foot six and have no problem with that. If a man is genuinely seven foot six, there are few people who want to make him five foot two. But people are very troubled by a five foot two person claiming that he is seven foot six because this robs them of some level of space of their common sense.

Consistent with certainty of a person's givens and the humility of concern as to how they are exploited, is a corresponding lack of space. It is an extraordinary thing that the more secure (and therefore humble) a person is, the less space he requires. The less secure a person is (and in whom there is a large *yeshus*), the more need there is to present to the world a false picture of abilities. The more space a person requires of those around him, the more they are in pain. The more secure a person is and the more *bittul* he has in his own position, the less space he requires — seven foot six or not his feet are not too big and his toes will be free from being trodden on.

The problem is that to climb the mountain of this book, we cannot seek to change others. The sweat of the climb is to effect *self-change*.

It is a great secret of Torah that the antidote to the pain inflictor is not to ask the offender to be content with less space but to require less oneself. This is a very deep requirement. There then is no awful person who is a space robber because there is no space to intrude upon.

The ability to take no space is *bittul; bittul* is *kedushah*. The ultimate example of *kedushah* was the *luchos* (tablets). Each tablet was some fifteen inches cubed in size. Yet they miraculously took no space in Holy of Holies in the Temple, being holiness by definition.

The conclusion suddenly becomes clear. In order to love a fellow Jew, there must be the opposite of hate. Hate comes from being cheated of space. If a person can diminish the space he himself requires, he will be subjected to less theft. *Bittul* allows for *ahavas Yisrael* because only then are the attempts to take space irrelevant.

In the absence of cause for hatred, there can be causeless love.

BUILDING BLOCK NO. 5

MITZVOS — LIMBS & SINEWS OF THE WORLD

Everything that was made in the six days of creation was made with a soul and a body. This is equally true of each of the levels of creation.[28]

There are four categories in physicality:

Domeim	—	inert matter
Tzomeiach	—	growing things, plants
Chai	—	animals
Medaber	—	those that can speak[29]

There is no gray area between any of these four categories. The four categories are entirely isolated from each other and everything created in the world belongs to one of the four categories.

We will see later that a secret of a Jew's mission in life is to elevate and refine himself through these categories.[30]

Every specie in each category has both a soul and a body. It is true that a soul is not so obvious in a stone or a tree as it is in a human being but it is there anyway. In exactly the same way, the whole of creation has a soul and a body. The soul (or spiritual aspects of the world) are connected to Torah and the body (or physical aspects of the world) to *mitzvos*.[31] *Mitzvos* are the 613 commandments that *Hashem* gave *Am Yisrael* at Mount Sinai.

It is explained in our oral tradition that the world is sustained by Jews learning Torah and Jews doing *mitzvos*. If Jews were to stop

---

28. See *Tanya*, Chapter 38.
29. See *Ibid*.
30. See for example *Likkutei Sichos*, Vol. 24, p. 643.
31. See *Tanya*, Chapters 23 & 37 and *Likkutei Sichos*, Vol. 3, p. 774.

learning Torah and doing *Mitzvos* for a moment, the world would cease to exist.[32] As we travel together, we will see the extraordinary logic of Jewish migration and its reason.

Here it is sufficient to note that *Chassidus* explains that Jews have never been permitted by *Hashem*, since we have been in Golus, to live together in one place. Being in different geographical locations has allowed those groups not subject to the decrees we have endured for thousands of years to sustain those presently persecuted. This sustenance is a result of the Torah being learned and the *mitzvos* being performed. In turn the world remains nourished.[33]

There are 613 *mitzvos* corresponding to 613 referent functions in the body. 248 positive *mitzvos* ("do's"), 365 negative *mitzvos* ("dont's") correspond to 248 "limbs" and 365 "sinews" in the human body.[34] The human body in microcosm, a small world, from which it is possible to observe and generalize about the larger spiritual and physical world.[35] In the same way as a Jew has a *neshomah* and a body, so to does the world have a *neshomah* and a body.

A secret to which we ordinary people are not privy is the eerie way in which a Rebbe is able to analyze a physical defect in a Jew. What is clear is that the physical is affected by the defective spiritual position of the person. A Rebbe, recognizing the *neshomah* of the person, is able to then in some way generalize the defect in the *mitzvah* which is causing the resultant physical problem.

Conversely, if there is no *mitzvah* problem relating to that limb or sinew, the Rebbe instructs ignoring medical advice to the gasp of onlookers. Stories of this are legion.

One Sydney woman, diagnosed with a huge brain tumor, sought advice from three specialists, two of whom said not to operate and one to do so. With a healthy fear of doctors and the knife, she took the advice of the majority and decided not to have

---

32. See *Shabbos* 87a.
33. See for example *Sefer HaMaamarim Kuntreisim* Vol. 1, p. 64ff.
34. See *Zohar*, Vol. 1, p. 170b; see also *Sefer HaSichos* 5741, Vol. 1, p. 305.
35. See *Midrash Tanchuma, Parshas Pekudei*.

the operation. Her daughters wrote to the Rebbe[36] asking for a *berochah* that, since she was not to have the operation, she should live a long, useful and healthy life. The Rebbe replied advising her *not* to listen to the doctors who said not to operate. She should have the operation and everything would be fine. The woman had the operation which was an entire success. Everything the doctors were worried about did not eventuate.

How can a Rebbe take such a responsibility? An uncaring person, let alone an ordinary person, would not be prepared to take the responsibility to advise someone to take a life decision choice of this kind. Who would do that? Who would take that responsibility? Not only once, but the Rebbe did repeatedly, daily, for members of *Am Yisrael* all over the globe. How could he do that? If he were guessing, sooner or later he would be wrong. What sort of human being would guess? What sort of human being would give advice in such circumstances?

The answer is the Rebbe is not guessing, he knows exactly. How does he know exactly? He knows exactly which *Mitzvah* is going wrong in relation to that function in the body which is physically sick. One of the members in our community, faced with amputation of one of his legs, asked the Rebbe for a *berochah* and the Rebbe's reply asked for his x-rays. When they were dispatched, the Rebbe replied they were not the subject's x-rays. A doctor reading this book will note that it is impossible to make a mistake with x-rays as the name is fused onto the photograph at the time it is taken. Nevertheless, the photographs were in fact not the person's x-rays.

How did the Rebbe know this? Obviously, we do not know but we can surmise this: because the 613 *Mitzvos* relate to 613 specific physical areas in the body, a Rebbe can analyze whether a limb is affected by an adversely conducted *Mitzvah*. Nowhere is it written which *Mitzvah* corresponds to which item in the body. This appears to be a secret *Tzaddikim* have. When something goes wrong physically, it is because a *Mitzvah* or group of *Mitzvos* are not being performed properly. The *koichus* (power) that should be flowing to

---

36. See notes on Lubavitcher Rebbes at end of the book.

that limb is subverted. The power that should be coming from the soul (Torah) to the physical body *(Mitzvos)* is not flowing properly.

Another example. There was a child in South Africa in kindergarten who used to wander out into the road. The supervisors were beside themselves as they could not prevent this child repeating this behavior. Attempts were made to punish the child, then to bribe the child positively but, at every opportunity, the child escaped into the street. Twice the child was lost and twice found. In desperation, the parents took advice from the Rebbe. The Rebbe told them to check the *mezuzahs* on their doors. They checked their *mezuzahs* and found that the word *"oovishorecho"* (your gates) was defective. They changed the *mezuzah* immediately and the child never walked out of the gate again. How does the Rebbe know that a child walking out of a gate in their case is related to the *mitzvah* of *mezuzah?* We do not know. That is a Rebbe's job. But we do know that the spiritual power flowing into physical activities flows out of Torah and down through *mitzvos.*

For many non-observant Jews, blindness is embraced. How many Jews are heard to say, confronted with a *mitzvah,* "I am not that religious". Friends with their own shins bruised nod in sage agreement.

Know that this Jew is still, from his perspective, close to *Hashem.* That is not in issue. Indeed, it is this very closeness which makes him go wrong. He believes G-d knows what is in his mind and will understand his limitations. In his heart, he is a good Jew and the fact that he does not keep the *mitzvah* is known to and conceded by *Hashem* because He understands individual weaknesses and He makes allowances. Familiar? All true but irrelevant.

Let us take the example of tuning in an amplifier. Badly tuned, there is a static response and an unclear signal. To receive the music clearly and beautifully, adjustment is as specific as possible — and with the best possible tuning equipment. This is precisely what happens with a *mitzvah.* There are people who are so scrupulous about their *mitzvos* that everything else in life is eclipsed. But there is nothing else in life. That is the point. What such Jews are doing is drawing down life force power from Torah into physicality through the *mitzvos* which they do.

A moment's reflection will lead to the realization that nothing a human being can do can in any way affect *Hashem*. So *Hashem* will have no benefit or detriment whether a man tunes in the signal clearly or poorly.[37] It then becomes clear that the person receiving the benefit of the scrupulous adherence of the *mitzvah* is the person who is doing the listening rather than the Sender of the signal. No difference exists in the source of the signal whether a radio is tuned in or it is not tuned in. This concern with doing *mitzvos* properly, completely and exactly is therefore a concern of each individual in particular and *Am Yisrael* at a more general level. Indeed, at its most general level, the whole world benefits the more clearly the signals are brought in.

---

37.   See *Job* 35:6-7.

BUILDING BLOCK NO. 6

NEFESH HABAHAMIS (ANIMAL SOUL)
NEFESH HOELOKIS (G-DLY SOUL)

Jews, as we shall see, are different from Gentiles. Jews have a spiritual purpose, Gentiles a physical one.[38] This can be compared to hands and feet.

Hands are different from feet. Not better, not worse. But certainly different. Although part of the same body of humanity, hands serve a different function than do feet. And if a hand is pressed to do the job of a foot, it will be uncomfortable, clumsy and unfulfilled.

Contrary to the hopes of our egalitarian society and legislation insisting on the sameness of men and women (let alone the sameness of people), the fact is that it is a secret of Torah that Jews are functionally different from non-Jews. This is not an easy concept to accept in the beginning of travels in Torah. We have been educated to believe a series of fictions in our generation, one of which is that there really are no differences between people. Clarifying this fiction should not be confused with the noble ideal of equal rights and opportunity for all. Nevertheless, man remains different from animal, man from woman and Jew from Gentile.

The Talmud categorizes Jews as different in levels of mercy, modesty and acts of goodness.[39]

Here, however, we need to understand a Jew's functional difference. As we proceed it will become obvious that, by appreciating the difference in purpose, a Jew can ultimately isolate and identify his purpose. Living consistently with his purpose makes a Jew fulfilled, satisfied and happy.

---

38.   See for example *Likkutei Sichos,* Vol. 25, p. 49.
39.   See *Yevamos* 79a.

A Jew is different in that he has a *neshomah*, an additional level to the life force of other human beings. This does not make him better or worse; just different, with different tasks and different responsibilities. A Jew, thinking and reacting as a Gentile, is guaranteed frustration and a life of bruised shins. An analysis of the *neshomah* will take place later in much more detail. Meanwhile, every Jew has the *nefesh* (life force) of every human being known as the *Nefesh HaBahamis* (Animal Soul). His additional soul, *neshomah*, is also known as the *Nefesh HoElokis* (G-dly Soul).[40]

There is nothing bad about the *Nefesh HaBahamis*. The *Nefesh HaBahamis* is interested in a natural, physical result.[41] So, for example, if a man is hungry, the *Nefesh HaBahamis* gives the man the drive to find food. If the needed food cannot be obtained, the signal from the *Nefesh HaBahamis* for food remains unabated. From the *Nefesh HoElokis*, the second soul, the *neshomah*, comes the brake on the *Nefesh HaBahamis*. It will signal a need to obtain the food in accordance with Torah. The Jekyl and Hyde syndrome in a Jew comes from the knowledge known to Jews for three and a half thousand years — that a Jew has a *Nefesh HaBahamis* which has *needs* and a *Nefesh HoElokis* which seeks to *control needs*, or wants and to refine the *Nefesh HaBahamis*.[42]

If our man is hungry and he cannot be satisfied with food because there is an obstacle in the way, the *Nefesh HaBahamis* activates the *seichel* (the intellect) to overcome that obstacle.[43] The need to overcome the obstacle is parve. It is not good, not bad, simply necessary.

If the obstacle is great enough, the *Nefesh HaBahamis* will rise to the occasion finally doing whatever is required to succeed. If theft is necessary, it will steal; if murder is necessary, it will kill. If however the *Nefesh HaBahamis* resolves to steal, kill or do other wrong, the *Nefesh HoElokis* will engage in battle with it. The moment there is a resolution to transgress a *mitzvah*, there is a

---

40. See *Tanya*, Chapters 1 & 2.
41. See *Tanya*, Chapter 8; *Likkutei Sichos*, Vol. 23, p. 139 footnote #46.
42. See *Tanya*, Chapter 37.
43. See *Tanya*, Chapter 6.

moral decision to be made. The *Nefesh HoElokis* will come into play and, depending on the relative strength of the person's *Nefesh HaBahamis*, it will either win or lose the battle.

An important reality is that it will win or lose simply as a result of training. The *Nefesh HoElokis* does not succeed automatically. Victory is a matter of training in exactly the same way as the human body can increase muscle by exercise. Everything physical is an extension of what exists in the spiritual.

The fact that something exists in the physical world is only because it is a spiritual truth. In the same way, the *Nefesh HoElokis* with exercise becomes stronger and the *Nefesh HaBahamis* denied exercise atrophies. This is why of course it is so vitally important to educate children in Torah from the very earliest possible moment, so that their *Nefesh HoElokis* becomes as vigorous as possible and their *Nefesh HaBahamis* remains as innocent as possible.

Now, although the *Nefesh HaBahamis* is parve, not bad, not good, the desire to overcome obstacles contrary to Torah is of course not good. Born from the *Nefesh HaBahamis* is the *yetzer hora* (Evil Inclination).[44] It is a fundamental cornerstone of Torah that every Jew (apart from very special people discussed later) has a *yetzer hora*. The *yetzer hora* means literally an inclination for bad. What does "bad" mean? "Bad" means contrary to Torah and *mitzvos*. Every Jew has a *yetzer hora* according to the strength of his *Nefesh HaBahamis*. The *Nefesh HaBahamis* is strong in everybody because they are born with a *Nefesh HaBahamis*.[45] The *Nefesh HoElokis* requires cultivation.[46] The *yetzer hora* will be as strong as a man is at any point of time in his life. The *Nefesh HoElokis* of a Jew spawns the *yetzer tov* (Good Inclination), the desire to do good. What does "good" mean? "Good" means learning Torah and doing *mitzvos*. Every Jew has a *yetzer tov*, part of the *Nefesh HoElokis*.

When a Jew therefore is confronted with a life problem, there will be functioning equally at the same moment, his *yetzer hora* and his *yetzer tov*. The *yetzer hora* functions so as to achieve

---

44. See *Or HaTorah, Balak* p. 1659-1661.
45. See *Sanhedrim* 91b.
46. See for example *Or HaTorah, Tehillim* p. 159.

whatever the need is at any given moment; if there is an obstacle which requires doing bad to overcome it, bad will be done.

If the obstacle requires bad to be done inventively, it will be done inventively. But always the *yetzer tov* has the potential to overcome the *yetzer hora* and ultimately even to turn it to do good. Curiously, the *Nefesh HoElokis* has the capacity to reveal itself instantly. If a person's *teshuvah* (return) is great enough, if a person's need for Torah is strong enough, we are promised that the *yetzer tov* can be called upon completely.[47] When this takes place, it becomes the total and effective brake on the *yetzer hora* resulting in real free choice in a Jew making moral decisions. Real free choice exists when the *yetzer tov* is as strong as the *yetzer hora*. There is the capacity in every Jew to succeed in overcoming his *yetzer hora* on all occasions and without fail.

Meanwhile, every man is tested until the day he dies; the more sophisticated he is, the more sophisticated will be his *yetzer hora*.[48] The more attention therefore must be given in cultivating his *yetzer tov*.

At a deeper level the *yetzer hora* is not an evil force in itself. Since everything created by *Hashem* is for good, ultimately the *yetzer hora* must be for good. It is for good because the point of the *yetzer hora* is to allow man to exercise free choice in order to grow and blossom.[49]

A Parable;

There was once a King whose only son was born with a birthmark. The King sent him, incognito, to the colonies. Before he left, the King cautioned his son on no account to gamble while away. The Prince swore to his father never to accept any kind of wager.

Successful in the colonies, the son ultimately made his way home, passing through a problem province. The Mayor of the province advocated a course of action contrary to the King's interest

---

47. See *Avodah Zorah* 17a.
48. See *Sukkah* 52a.
49. See *Tanya*, end of Chapter 9.

and so of course the Prince objected. The Prince and Mayor argued until at last the Prince who could withhold his patience no longer revealed his identity and required obedience from the Mayor. The Mayor challenged his authenticity, wagering one thousand rubles that the young man was not the Prince. One thousand rubles! The Prince remembered his promise to his father but this, after all, was certain. He accepted the bet, showed his birthmark and, of course, collected the thousand rubles.

When the Prince arrived home, he found the King devastated.

"How could you do it?", asked the King. "You swore to me you wouldn't take a bet. You swore."

"This is different." replied the Prince. "First of all, the disagreement related to your sovereignty. Secondly, I couldn't lose the bet."

"Fool." replied the King. "I bet the Mayor a million rubles you wouldn't accept."

The King is *Hashem* and, of course, the son is *Am Yisrael*. The Mayor is the *yetzer hora*. The *yetzer hora* is the tester of whether one triumphs in his potential for growth or the reverse. It is critical to see that although the Mayor has the short term reward of winning the bet, his love for the King makes him disappointed at the failure of his Prince. Always the rewards are greater for the triumph of the *yetzer tov* — although not always immediately obvious.

BUILDING BLOCK NO. 7

FROM WHERE IS THE SIGNAL COMING? YETZER HORA OR YETZER TOV?

Clearly, there must be a guide for a Jew to be able to determine whether a signal is coming from his *yetzer tov* or whether the signal is coming from his *yetzer hora*. At one end of the spectrum recognition is easy. Obviously, if a man desires to steal, it is not difficult to identify that signal as coming from his *yetzer hora*. More subtly, if a man makes the decision to learn Torah every morning at a fixed time, the suggestion to stay in a warm bed on a cold gray morning and miss learning can also be identified as coming from the *yetzer hora*.

But sometimes, on the other end of the spectrum, the message can be very unclear and the signal can come in a most seductive form;[50] for example, is the desire to cheat an insurance company really stealing?

Given that theft is forbidden, it requires a person of acumen to identify his *yetzer hora* here. After all, purrs that *yetzer hora*, adding to the list of stolen items is natural: Every insurance company expects it: They never pay the whole claim anyway: Obviously, the answer is to over claim. On the other hand, the signal not to cheat clearly comes from the *yetzer tov*. The *yetzer tov* will tell a man, if he will only listen, that it cannot be possible to profit when doing something contrary to *Hashem's* will. If He says not to steal, any extra money received from the insurance claim will be dissipated on negative matters such as doctors' bills.

There are even more subtle positions. We learn the *yetzer hora* attacks at the level it is best able to achieve success. A simple man

---

50.   See for example *Likkutei Sichos*, Vol. 16, p. 553.

will be attacked at a primitive level. A sophisticated scholar will be attacked on an ingeniously learned level.

There are a few tests; the first relates to *time*. Chassidim tell the story[51] of a pauper who explains to a Rebbe in private of his desperate need for three hundred rubles to marry off his daughter. Later the same day, amazingly another *Chosid* donated three hundred rubles to the Rebbe. The Rebbe's assistant was excited to see the donation as he realized that he could now pay the Rebbe's debts. When, however, he asked for the money, the Rebbe refused. A few moments later, the Rebbe suspended visitors and after some time elapsed called back the assistant. He instructed him to find the man in need of the three hundred rubles and to pay the money to him. The assistant was disappointed but the Rebbe's behavior was not altogether unexpected. But why the suspension of visitors and the delay?

Ultimately the Rebbe explained;

"There was never a question of keeping any of the money for myself or my debts. The question, was should the man who needed to marry off his daughter be given the whole three hundred rubles when, after all, this is a poor community and many people are desperately in need. There were at least three hundred families who could do very well with a ruble each at the moment. Should I give the whole three hundred rubles to one man to marry off his daughter or should I distribute the amount to bring relief to a considerable number of poor families?

To make this decision, I needed to decide from where the idea of distributing one ruble to three hundred deserving families was coming from. Was it coming from the *yetzer hora* or the *yetzer tov*?".

The Rebbe explained that, upon deep reflection, it was coming from his *yetzer hora*. Why? Because it was his second thought even though good in itself.

---

51.   Quoted in *A Treasury of Chassidic Tales On the Torah Vol. II by R.S.Y. Zevin* p. 532.

So here we have a test. The Rebbe's first inclination was to give the whole three hundred rubles to the man who needed to marry off his daughter. Only later did he give himself the alternative.

We know that when, in the attempt to do some good, a decision is made, the *yetzer hora* will attack that decision at that man's level. At what level can the *yetzer hora* attack a great man? Somewhere at least sophisticated enough for there to be a *choice* for him. One test of where the signal comes from therefore is that it comes *second* in time after and to undermine the first, good decision.

A second test relates to *motive*. There is a famous story about a snuff box. People used to use snuff, and snuff boxes to Chassidim in olden times, were like expensive pens to lawyers. The richer you were, the better your snuff box. The story goes that Shimon, a very rich man, was in shul one night when Reuven, a very poor man, asked Shimon for some snuff.

Producing a wonderful jewel-encrusted snuff box, Shimon took some snuff for himself and dismissed Reuven empty-handed in a rude and uncaring manner. It later happened that Shimon became poor and Reuven rich. Shimon went to a Rebbe to ask why he had become impoverished. The Rebbe reminded him of the incident of the snuff box. Once reminded, Shimon asked what he could do to once again be rich. The *Tzaddik* told him there were two ways. The first was to engineer Reuven to do to him what he had done to Reuven before. There was another way but he would not explain. Shimon sought out Reuven who was in the process of marrying off his daughter and who no longer recognized the disheveled Shimon. In the middle of the greatest moments of rejoicing when father was dancing with his son-in-law on a table, Shimon pulled at Reuven's trousers.

"What do you want?"

"Excuse me, can I have some snuff?"

"Now?"

"Now!"

Reuven descended from the table and, incredibly, he produced the very same bejeweled snuff box!

"Take as much as you want," said Reuven. Shimon burst out crying when his much disturbed host inquired after his strange behavior. Shimon told him all. His host listened carefully and then asked, "Why do you want me to be poor again? Before, when I was poor, you were content. When I am rich, you want me to be poor." Shimon now understood that the second way for him, not explained by the Rebbe, included not wishing poverty on Reuven. He no longer wanted his money back. He wanted other money. The end of the story was that Reuven made a deal with Shimon that he would support Shimon on a salary for the rest of his life and marry off all his children on one condition; that Shimon no longer would want his money back from Reuven. The deal was done and everybody lived happily. Because he repented sufficiently *teshuvah,* Shimon was once again entitled to have a certain amount of money. Again however there are the two signals. The signal to Shimon that he wanted *his* money back was a signal from his *yetzer hora* because it was at the expense of Reuven.

When he reached the level where the signal was coming from his *yetzer tov,* where *any* money would do him while meanwhile welcoming his friend's good fortune, Shimon then received enough.

There is a third and ultimate test of action;

Does the signal bring a man to doing positive good in actual fact or is the result no activity? If, for example, there is the potential to do *mitzvah* "A" or *mitzvah* "B", if neither is performed, long learned argument about which *mitzvah* is preferred must be coming from the *yetzer hora*[52]. If in fact one or, even better, both *mitzvos* are performed, the signal has come from the *yetzer tov.* We know this because the net result is the doing of the *mitzvos* in actuality. As a result more good has been brought into the world. This, after all, is the purpose of the *yetzer tov,* and the only ultimate clue to its signal.

52.   See for example *Likkutei Sichos,* Vol. 23, p. 473.

BUILDING BLOCK NO. 8

THE SECRET OF EXILE & REDEMPTION

This Building Block is so important, a short summary to this point is necessary.

We have learned about *Hashgochah Protis*, that the world is Divinely controlled in all areas except for moral decisions where human beings have been delegated free choice — Jews in relation to 613 matters and non-Jews in relation to 7 matters. We have learned that Jews are functionally different from non-Jews in that they have a *neshomah*, a part of G-d Himself; the *neshomah* undergoes a descent into the body for the purpose of an ascent higher than the level it was before its descent. We learned that this can be generalized to the world that every descent is for a purpose of an ascent; consequentially, in daily physical life, there are no descents without there being a corresponding, potential ascent.

We also learned that the task of each *neshomah* in every generation is to achieve that ascent by overcoming certain tests which are set against a background of difficulty. By overcoming these tests while being tossed around by those difficulties, the *neshomah* achieves its ascent to Paradise.

We also learned that every *neshomah* is in every body particularly and in a specific environment generally which is perfect for its job. If the mission were different, the environment would be different. If its tests are of wealth, the environment will be opulent, if of poverty, the environment will be meager.

Finally, know as *daas* that every environment is structured by G-d's kindness because it provides each *neshomah* the best chance for its success.

We then need one more notion to understand this vital Building Block. Torah is Eternal. What does that mean?

Torah is the wisdom of *Hashem* and, being so, it is unchangeable and eternal.

At a simple level, laws are immutable.[53] But this is only the tip of the iceberg of its meaning. Much more deeply, Torah is eternal in that it applies to every Jew in every generation, in every year, in every week, in every day, in every moment, precisely and constantly.

If there is a story in Torah, that story is equally a series of ever deeper levels. Firstly, there is the historical fact of it having happened. Avraham actually took his son and bound him thinking he was to be sacrificed. At the next level, the test of Avraham is a test that a Jew faces, on one way or another, in every generation. The details of the whole story are plumblines of every Jew's test of self-sacrifice in every generation.

Although it is so that the most prominent revelation of this will occur in the week the Torah portion applies,[54] it will also be relevant to every Jew every day. Revealed or concealed, Avraham's test will be pertinent daily.

One of the most important tides which ebb and flow in Torah for Jews in general, and for every Jew in particular, is the concept of *Mitzrayim* (bondage) and *geulah* (redemption). This concept is so important that we mention it in davening (prayer) every day. "*Mitzrayim*", although translated in English as "Egypt", in Hebrew connotes bondage, enclosure, crushed by rigid boundaries.[55] "Redemption" is described as our exodus from there.

Apart from being the name of a place, "*Mitzrayim*" refers to a state of a Jew. *Chassidus* teaches a Jew to tune into what is happening to himself on a daily basis; one of the things that are happening is the process of exile and redemption.

Exile and redemption connote this: there is a time in Jewish life where a Jew finds himself boxed in, trapped. There is then a process

---

53. See *Rambam, Hilchos Yesodei HaTorah* Chapter 9.
54. See *HaYom Yom,* Entry 2 Cheshvan.
55. See for example *Likkutei Sichos,* Vol. 2, p. 348ff.

by which a Jew can escape that bondage — an exodus from a state of spiritual, mental and physical servitude. The "exodus", as it is called, is a process which goes on every day. The process is reflected in Torah in a series of events. Those events, although they actually happened in history, keep happening until the final redemption — which will be the final entry into the land of Israel.[56]

At a deeper level, the process of exile into and redemption from *Mitzrayim* (Egypt) into the desert was repeated as exile into and redemption from the desert into Israel; exile from and redemption back to Israel at the time of the second Temple; the present exile and soon the final redemption.[57] This has been our pattern and, within that pattern, are a series of smaller sequences. The more particular smaller patterns belong to every Jew every day of his life.

The vision of Torah as being applicable daily and understanding the pattern of exile and redemption in particular lights up the darkness of daily confusion through these glasses. Looking with the spectacles of *Chassidus* allows a man to be able to understand the various periods of exile and redemption in his own life.

What does exile mean? The Rebbe gives the example of one who is sick. Cure requires two stages:[58] First is to recognize the sickness. Then only is diagnosis and cure possible. Without a person being conscious of his sickness, there can be no cure.

The sickness example, as it pertains to exile, illustrates the period in time and/or place where the revelation of G-dliness is not apparent.[59] In *Mitzrayim* (Egypt) there was no revelation of G-dliness.

When Israel left for the desert, they were accompanied by the Clouds of Glory, the Pillar of Fire and the Manna — all demonstrable evidence of revealed G-dliness.

Then, having left the desert for Israel, we were crowned with the Temple in which there was a heightened level of revelation. Ten

---

56. See *Ibid.*
57. See *Sefer HaMaamarim Melukot* Vol. 1, p. 121.
58. See *HaYom Yom,* Entry 16 Sivan.
59. See *Toraso Shel Moshiach* p. 1.

miracles occurred daily for all to marvel and experience.[60] Exile into Babylonia brought again the lack of revelation of G-dliness. The return to Israel and the Second Temple re-established an obvious presence of G-dliness. Now this exile, the longest historically, is also the darkest. This darkness is a process which increases until the dawn of Moshiach. Everything physical, as we have said, is a parable of that which is spiritual. The account of the creation of the world begins with evening, then morning, one day. Dark precedes light.[61] Night gives way to day in the physical because dark gives way to light in the spiritual.

It is astonishing and difficult to assimilate as *daas* that the production of that light is the charge of *neshomos* in every generation. The process of producing the light to eradicate the final darkness has taken two thousand years. We know from the Rebbe that the work is complete.[62]

We are here, moments before the final redemption, and in these last moments the darkness is most intense. Children set tramps alight in parks while they sleep, youths are beating their elders to death, streets are awash with blood let by muggers and rapists. With all modern technology we have achieved, people bar up their homes like jails, living in quiet stress from fear of their neighbors.

In physicality, darkness is deepest immediately before dawn; this is dictated by what happens spiritually. Jews have the capacity to end this darkness and bring light to their and everyone's lives.

As we have learned, Torah is immutable. A dazzling example of this is shown by the Rebbe[63] from the Torah sentence[64] describing the desert: "In the great and awesome desert with snakes, fiery serpents and scorpions, and thirst, where there was lack of water." The description is the physical manifestation of the spiritual state of desert.

---

60.   See *Ethics of Our Fathers* 5:5.
61.   See *Genesis* 1:5.
62.   See *Toraso Shel Moshiach* p. 8ff.
63.   See *Likkutei Sichos*, Vol. 2, p. 374.
64.   See *Deuteronomy* 8:15.

Taking the quote word-by-word, it illustrates a Jew's personal journey into exile. First, what is a great desert? When a Jew faces his non-Jewish surroundings and sees them as great compared to his private environment, he takes the first step into exile. Here is the first step into the desert. When a Jew decides that he is numerically inferior (true) and therefore his power to influence for the good is inferior (not true) and that the significance of his task is being minimized, he confirms that first step. The belief that the surroundings are so great that they rule over Israel is mental exile.

The next adjective describing "desert" is "awesome". This is the trembling Jew taking his second step into exile. Regarding the desert as great, a Jew becomes ashamed and afraid of his own position. There are of course various levels of shame. There are Jews whose shame makes them want to melt with their host cultures. There are Jews who present themselves to the outside world as non-Jewish as possible but who wish to maintain some kind of historical continuity. Then there are those prepared to be observant in their own home when the door is closed; they will come home and put on a *yarmulke,* have their children say a *berochah* or two, even go to shul but always in cringing shame of the non-Jewish environment. The next level reluctantly follows the pattern that has been laid out for them, wearing a *yarmulke* and *tzitzis* under sufferance and discomfort whenever in a public place. In exile, all these levels of shame are possible. In Israel, no Jew cares. When a Jew does not care, he is in spiritual Israel, redeemed.

"Snakes" is the next word of the verse. Snake bite is accompanied by fierce body heat. This is the level of enthusiasm of a *neshomah* which is misdirected. The enthusiasm is sapped making money, accumulating pleasures or toys, creating power and all the other compulsive pursuits with which we are all familiar. The poor *neshomah*, instead of teaching the *Nefesh HaBahamis* how to fly, is made to grovel by it in the gutter of physical distractions.

The next step into exile is very deep indeed. The venom of the scorpion is cold. Cold is a plane lower than heat. At least enthusiasm can be rechanneled for good. Indifference however is next to death.

The final desperate level is thirst without water. Water, in the Holy Writings, is an analogy for Torah. So when, for instance, Yosef was thrown into the pit, it is described as being filled with scorpions, then there is the incredible account of there being no water in the pit. When a Jew has no water (Torah), he is thirsty. This is a terrible state for a Jewish *neshomah*. A *neshomah* thirsts naturally for Torah. Denied it, a Jew will seek all kinds of other liquid to quench his thirst; for a Jew, such other liquids cannot succeed. There is an extraordinarily high frequency of Jews in cults — only because their *neshomos* have been denied the elixir of their life which is Torah.

So how then do Jews escape exile? How can they burst through the boundaries of *Mitzrayim* and fill their lungs and hearts with the pure fresh air of freedom?

We will learn the answer together as we journey but meanwhile the important preparation is to see the ebb and flow of daily difficulty as a barometer of the service of one's *neshomah*. *Feel* that all boundaries are from outside; all can be smashed like toothpicks from the inside. As we learn together, the how will become evident.

PART TWO
LIFE SECRETS

LIFE SECRETS — CHAPTER 1

SIMCHAH (JOY)

A seemingly impossible and certainly difficult requirement of Torah is that a Jew serve *Hashem* with *simchah* (joy);[65] How often are we to be *b'simchah* (joyful)? It appears the requirement is constant. Who can be joyful all the time? What about the irritations and frustration of daily life? Nevertheless, as *Hashem* will never test people with what they cannot do, it is not only possible but eminently achievable to be joyful all the time. Both here and later in this book, we will learn how together. Meanwhile, there is some important prerequisite information.

As mentioned (in Building Block No. 2), *Hashem* blesses every *neshomah* with a combination of three separate *berachos*. One is health, one is children and one is *parnossah* (sustenance). Very few Jews merit, for whatever reason, to have all three *berachos* at all times in their life in the way they would like. The most a Jew is usually permitted is two. More rarely, he receives one and sometimes, unusually, none. There are some apparently unfortunate people who have bad health, who are bankrupt and who have no children or no nachas from those children they do have. For these people the tests are very difficult. Even where one has all three *berachos,* it is unusual to find all three available at one time.

The astonishing thing about the requirement of being *b'simchah* (joyful) is that it does not apply only to those Jews who are lucky enough to have all three *berachos*. It is a requirement for every Jew irrespective of whether he has any of the *berachos*! Even people with some experience in *Chassidus* find this a difficult thing to take on board so that it becomes their private perspective (*daas*).

---

65. See *Psalms* 100:3.

Happiness is an aspect of being *b'simchah*. Society teaches us from our earliest moments however, that happiness is dependent on what we accumulate or how physically capable we are or whether our children will act out our unfulfilled dreams through their achievements. If a man does not possess any or all of those things, it is axiomatic in Western culture that he is therefore deprived. Being deprived, he in fact feels miserable — the opposite of *simchah*. Without matching BMW's and $10 million worth of assets, we cannot have the resources to be happy because happiness is dependent on these very resources.

Furthermore, it is apparently obvious that Shimon who is rich, healthy and has nachas from his children is better off than Reuven who is bankrupt, sick and has rebellious children. It seems axiomatic that Shimon is going to be more *b'simchah* and indeed happier than Reuven.

Extraordinarily, a Jewish *neshomah* has the obligation to be *b'simchah* even without any of those *berachos,* G-d forbid. How is it possible to adhere to this cardinal principle of Jewish life in a traffic jam, in planning and being disappointed in a business deal, in hospital and, G-d forbid, when children are sick?[66]

We will learn this very deep secret together by reference to what we have learned already. Every Jewish *neshomah* undergoes a *yeridah*, a descent into its body, in order to afford it the opportunity to do one or more specific jobs. These tasks have to do with refining the body and the *Nefesh HaBahamis*, and elevating the surrounding environment. The process of refinement and elevation can only be accomplished by each *neshomah* in its precisely suitable environment.

So if the highest point of greatness a *neshomah* can achieve in one *gilgul* is from poverty, then it is an act of *chesed*, an act of kindness for *Hashem* to organize the man's affairs so that he is without money. For the duration of his life, no matter how he tries, no matter his standard of education, how many jobs he works at or how many business deals he attempts, he will remain without

---

66. See *Berachos* 54a, "One is obligated to bless *Hashem* on bad tidings just like he blesses *Hashem* on the good".

money. Of course, this *chesed* is not understood. People spend their lives cursing their bad fortune when in reality they have the precise and perfect fortune for their specific need. Conversely, a man to be tested with money may be the most apparently undeserving recipient — but whatever he does will turn to gold. The opportunity to be catapulted to the stars, to fulfill his tests, may come in the personification of a filthy beggar seeking help, or the building of a new *Yeshivah*. The point is that his environment will be perfect for his specific tests.

We have learned that the three *berachos* are beyond the control of a Jew. Effort is required to make the vessel. But this is the only contribution we make. Whether the chance for our *aliyah* is from wealth or poverty, it is *Hashem's* kindness which provides that forum in which to function.

Needless to say, just as we are tested as individuals in each *gilgul*, *Am Yisrael* is tested in each generation. There are generations which are rich, those which are poor; there are times of peace and times of stress. Always the *Hashgochah Protis* is for our benefit.

Why then are we encouraged to pray for change? A man dying does not have to accept this as only an act of *chesed*, the best environment for his *neshomah*, and go ahead and die. He can, and indeed according to *Halachah* (Jewish law) must, ask *Hashem* to *change* his position.[67]

Meanwhile for a Jew the best chance to improve any of the three *berachos* and all of them is to learn Torah and do *mitzvos*.[68] The next chapter will discuss the *parnossah* for a Jew. The best way for him to have good children is to have a home which is a Torah home. And the best way for him to be healthy in body is to be healthy in spirit, i.e. in living consistently with *Hashem's* will. It is an absolute waste of time to wish to substitute one person's environment with another's.

---

67. See *Berachos* 10a.
68. See *Rosh HaShanah* 16b.

If the man next door has a Ferrari for every one of his teenage children and an indoor and outdoor swimming pool and whatever else we believe we need for our happiness, we now see this is not so. It takes years of learning this and a lifetime of *Chassidus* to be able to understand that the environment we have is perfect for our life and the man next door has the perfect environment for his. The desire to change therefore, gradually disappears as this perspective becomes *daas* (See Building Block No. 3).

Obviously, if a person is short of money and needs to fix his children's teeth, he will feel pain at some level at his inability to supply the money. The pain however cannot affect the recognition that his *neshomah* is presently in a perfect position to do its job generally.

The recognition of this brings a man to joy. The realization that one is perfectly placed is a joyful realization. Not just once in a lifetime; not just a shaft of light occasionally realizing the *neshomah* to be perfectly placed, but every day. Every day when the bank is pressing or when the deal goes wrong.

We are going to be tested very day. Let us understand this. It is a generalization for every Jewish *neshomah*. A Jew cannot get out of bed and be free of tests. If the test was passed yesterday, there will be a brand new set of tests today. Always however these tests are perfect for the respective *neshomah* and therefore a cause for joy.

Why joy? Even if the environment is perfect, why joy? It has to be understood that each test is a potential for growth and every time adversity is overcome there is spiritual growth. Indeed, we learn that a man should try and turn down the volume on his needs for physicality and turn up the volume on his needs for spirituality. In spirituality, the more one has, the better one is. In physicality, the more one has, the harder it can be. So ironically the more of those three *berachos* a person has, the harder could become his spiritual development. It is much easier for a man living on bread and water and sleeping on the floor in Jerusalem who has never seen a movie to learn Torah than a person brought up in the Eastern Suburbs of Sydney awash with money and the capacity for every distraction.

Realizing one's position is a perfect potential to be able to complete his *neshomah's* mission in life and therefore attain its *aliyah*, a lifelong process. It is so important that ultimately a man can reach the level that he can in sincerity make a *berochah* (a blessing) on adversity. According to Jewish law, we make *berachos* when, G-d forbid, things go wrong. We bless *Hashem* for being just. Without *Chassidus* this is incomprehensible. With *Chassidus* we do understand it. The *berochah* is this; *Hashem* is providing the perfect environment for the *neshomah* to have its potential for its *aliyah*. We cannot see it at the moment? We are not looking. Put on the binoculars of *Chassidus*.

There is one other point. There is a legitimate human emotion in grief. At first glance from what we have learned, this should not be. As everything is divinely controlled with *Hashgochah Protis*, and as every *neshomah* is in its perfect environment with the maximum potential for a *neshomah's aliyah*, and recognizing that must make us *b'simchah*, then how come we cry? Why sit shiva when a relative dies? Why do we have laws on mourning? There are *Halachos*[69] that say how sad we have to be for the first seven days, for the next thirty days, and then ultimately for the remaining eleven months.

Hashem created man with certain psychological needs and those needs, when denied, are accompanied by pain. If an appendix malfunctions there is pain. The pain is a signal. The pain allows us to recognize and then fix an appendix. Pain is a necessary part of life and part of the psychological process with which we have been created. Still, it must be contained within boundaries.[70] So when a father dies, G-d forbid, the level of mourning is controlled. There is a week when we mourn at a certain level and then there is change to a different level of mourning for a further thirty days and finally change for the next eleven months. After the twelfth month, mourning is completed and indeed forbidden.

It is forbidden to mourn on Shabbos — even in the seven days. There was no greater *Chosid* of any Rebbe than the Rebbe of the Previous Rebbe. The Previous Rebbe passed away on Shabbos and

---

69.   See *Shulchan Aruch, Yoreh De'ah* 340:8.
70.   See *Igros Kodesh of the Rebbe*, Vol. 17, p. 162.

the old Chassidim who still remember report that the Rebbe did not exhibit the slightest difference in behavior on that Shabbos as compared to any other Shabbos. For a *Tzaddik* who is living tissue of *Hashem's* will, the *Halachah* is paramount.

Shabbos overrides mourning so the Rebbe was *b'simchah* as on any Shabbos. The moment Shabbos came out, the moment *Havdalah* was said, the Rebbe broke down.[71] Similarly, when his wife, the *Rebbetzin,* died, the Rebbe cried publicly. When it came Shabbos, the Rebbe *farbrenged* as usual, waved his hands as usual and everyone sang as usual.

So then, what *method* is available to a man to focus on realizing his position is perfect all the time?

The answer comes from a great secret of Torah implicit in all the above. Happiness and one's environment are actually unrelated! If this where not so, *Hashem* would not require all Jews to be equally joyful without giving them equal blessings and surroundings. It must be the *simchah* that is a *state of mind.*[72] It must also be that that state of mind can be absolutely controllable by each of us with effort and training irrespective of our environment. And so it is. We pray that *Hashem* improve our *berachos* because we pray for the test to be over.

Until his position is changed by such prayer, understanding the mechanics of this controlled joy removes a Jew totally from the apparently random choppy sea of daily existence. Where the mind is *b'simchah* and steady in its *emunah* (faith), there is light and warmth with the best view in the world. To enjoy it takes time and effort — living any other way takes more.

---

71. See *Yemei Bereishis* p. 67 onwards.
72. On the methods to bring oneself to that state of mind see *Tanya,* Chapter 26ff.

LIFE SECRETS — CHAPTER 2

PARNOSSAH
(FINANCIAL SUSTENANCE)

We begin with a saying from the Talmud familiar to all *Chabad* children; If a person says, "I strived and failed" — don't believe him. "I didn't strive and succeeded" — don't believe him. "I strived and succeeded" — believe him. [73]

The Rebbe has explained — and the whole of this section is based on that explanation the concept of *parnossah* (financial sustenance). Jewish *parnossah* appears at first glance to contradict this section of Talmud. We will see however that this is of course not so.

The wording of the Torah in relation to work and Shabbos is that "in six days your work shall be done and the seventh day will be for you a holy day, a Shabbos on which to withdraw from mundane pursuits." [74] An important distinction needs to be understood; a Jew's *parnossah* and a non-Jew's *parnossah* is entirely different and this section is restricted to Jewish *parnossah*.

The wording does not say, "you will work." It says, "your work shall be done" in a passive sense. [75] The Hebrew word, "your work shall be done", is a passive word. Can we therefore say that all we have to do is to exist, and we will have *parnossah?* Clearly this cannot be true because the world is so designed that everything in nature requires the participation of man. The first statements in Torah make clear that the world is created, and we are put on the world to complete the work of creation. There are various worlds, as we shall see elsewhere but in this, the physical world, the lowest of all possible worlds, there is a partnership between *Hashem* and

---

73. See *Megillah* 6b.
74. See *Shemos* 35:2.
75. For the following explanation see *Likkutei Sichos,* Vol. 1, p. 187ff.

mankind. Clearly, therefore, one cannot simply sit believing what will be will be and what won't be won't be. We know this is wrong because Torah directs our intervention into that partnership. As far as work is concerned although the word is passive, involvement is required — passive involvement. Six days a week, the work has to be done but the perspective of a Jew is that that work is passive, that he is as it were grudgingly doing it.

Now the Torah also says:

"Strive with hands in order to be able to eat, and you will be happy and it will be good for you."[76]

The simple meaning of this is the directive not to be a beggar. Man should work for himself and be independent and not be a burden on the community.

The deeper level is that one is required to work with one's hands not one's head or one's heart. A Jew's head is his *seichel*, his intellect, and his heart is his *middos*, his emotion. These must be reserved for Torah and *mitzvos*. Only then can he be truly happy. One must strive with the hands, and then he will eat and then he will be happy and it will be good for him. When will he be happy and it be good for him? Only when working with the hands, not with the head, not with the heart.

No stress. Why no stress? No head, no heart. Where is the head and the heart? Learning Torah, doing *mitzvos*. What is the primary job? The primary job is to be a Jew who learns Torah and does his *mitzvos*. What is the secondary begrudged job? Earning a living with the hands. Reserve *seichel* for Talmud. Reserve *middos* for learning to be good to others, loving and being kind to a wife and learning to be good to enemies and all those irritating people who keep treading on one's feet which may be too big.

Incidentally, the second quote lists two happinesses; happy and good for you. This means happy in this world and it will be good for you in the World to Come.[77] If one does not work with one's head and one's heart, not only will there be more happiness here but life will be easier in the World to Come — in *Gan Eden*.

---

76. See *Psalms* 128:2.
77. See *Ethics of Our Fathers* 4:1.

This is what the notion of passivity about the work being done means. For six days there is no question that a Jew must work. But only that which is necessary.

What is necessary? Unfortunately, there is no fixed measure for this. Everyone has to manage this calculation alone.

How can a person approach his business like that? Let us understand that we have all grown up in a host society where *parnossah* is a sacred cow. The Torah is eternal and applies in all aspects to every generation. Egyptians worshipped the Nile as a false god. Pharaoh threw Jewish children into the Nile. *Chassidus* teaches that the modern Pharaoh throwing Jewish children into the Nile is society throwing Jewish children into a pursuit of *parnossah* which eclipses any real perspective of life.[78]

The Torah also says that *"Hashem* your G-d will bless you in everything that you do."[79] Now, who is doing the blessing? It is that *Hashem* will bless you in everything you do. Does the *berochah* (blessing) of *parnossah* come from us or from *Hashem?* Every Jew must make this decision.

If a man believes that *parnossah* comes from him, he has an excellent reason for throwing his head and his heart into the process of earning it, and earning more. How does he obtain more? — by working harder.

He will lie awake at night, he will worry and he will plan, calculating and artfully dodging. People fall in love with this disease until their life is wasted. The head and heart is involved to the exclusion of everything else.

When the words of the Torah are understood for what they say, namely, that the *berochah* comes from *Hashem*, your G-d, and who "will bless you in everything that you do", there is a whole and dramatic change in perspective. If the *berachos* come from *Hashem* and not as the product of one's effort, a man would be a fool for investing his head and heart into the labor. What a waste of energy this is! Would a man guaranteed $1,000.00 next week irrespective of his effort, work? Even if so, how hard? Would he kill himself? He

---

78.   See *Likkutei Sichos,* Vol. 1, p. 111.
79.   See *Deuteronomy* 15:18.

may work but only to establish a connection between himself and being paid.

How much more so would this be true if he knew he would not earn any more by investing emotional effort. Who would kill themselves for nothing if their *parnossah* was anyway fixed?[80]

Here is a secret of Torah;

What brings *parnossah* to a Jew is the *berochah* from *Hashem*. Therefore, the question becomes only, what needs to be done in order to obtain that *berochah?* This becomes the only concern. Clearly, one of the things *not* necessary is to put the head and the heart into the enterprise.

But then why work at all? Why not go to shul and learn, daven and go out into the street and try to help people all day? In fact, can't we say that working is a sign of lack of *emunah* (faith)? If the *berochah* is from *Hashem* and *Hashem* is going to sustain us, can't we leave it to Him? We learn elsewhere in this book that the whole purpose of the *neshomah* being sent down into a Jewish body is to learn Torah and do *mitzvos* and to so make a dwelling place for G-d in the lowest of all possible worlds. If *Hashem* designs this plan, He cannot allow us to starve, and therefore maybe we should not work at all?

It is the way of *Hashem* that His blessing must flow down in a natural way. For whatever reason, it is His requirement that, even when nature is suspended, the suspension is through nature and in a way which is apparently natural. In order to receive the blessing, man must make a *keli* (vessel) to contain that *berochah*.[81] The vessel must be part of nature so that the *berochah* devolves through apparently natural means. The *keli* for *parnossah* is work. This is the reason, and the sole reason, a Jew is required to work.

The wording we referred to in the Torah also really connotes toil. When a person does what he loves to do, he does not get tired. A person tires quickly from what he hates. A Jewish *neshomah*, no matter how it is covered up, fundamentally desires to learn Torah

80. See *HaYom Yom*, Entry 4 Menachem Av.
81. See *Likkutei Sichos*, Vol. 1 p. 216.

and do *mitzvos*. A Jewish *neshomah* thirsts for Torah. Everything else becomes work, toil.

What about all those people who love work; they are successful making money and they love to work. Let us understand; there is nothing wrong with making plenty of money. Indeed only a fool denies this, so some people not only love work, they want to multiply the effort and the time spent working. Sadly, some successful people become so involved that when they have more money than they can spend in a thousand years, they still must work — because otherwise they have nothing to do! In other words, what is basically a curse has become a consuming need. The tail has begun to wag the dog. Work is a curse given to us as a result of the sin with the fruit of the tree. The poor person who lives in order that he should work is to be pitied in his lack of understanding.

So what must a Jew do? Every man therefore must make a vessel according to his level. This vessel must begin with a Jew's understanding of his identity. There was a Chassid of the Previous Lubavitcher Rebbe who was asked whether he was a lawyer. "Certainly not," he replied, "I am a Jew whose *parnossah* comes to me through the vehicle of the legal profession." The primary perspective is that a person is a Jew whose *neshomah* has descended into his body to fulfill his purpose in this world. If the purpose is being fulfilled, there is a guarantee; *Hashem* says it will be good for you and you will be happy. It will be good for you in this world, it will be good for you in the next world, you will have no worries, and will overcome all problems. As we have seen, every *neshomah* has just what it needs to do its job.

Does all the above mean a man can forget work and simply play? Then even the hands are not in it. The head and the heart are not there, but the hands are not there either. Hands need to be in the office, to pick up the telephone, to do the mail. Allowing *parnossah* to take over one's being however and permitting it the central perspective of one's life is throwing life away into the Nile.

Finally, as to the size of the vessel, there is a concluding aspect. The size of the vessel seems to vary with a man's spiritual level. It is an incredible thing that for those people on a high enough level, the vessel may be extremely small. As we shall see in Chapter 7 on the

Secrets of the Festivals, R. Shimon Bar Yochai, who wrote the *Zohar,* spent thirteen years in a cave with his son buried to their necks in sand.[82]

Theoretically, they should have died of exposure and starvation. But for a *Tzaddik* that cave happened to have a stream running past it and a carob tree outside. Being perfect *Tzaddikim,* they had almost no burden of work for their sustenance. On the other hand, men of lesser stature in the mistaken belief that they were *Tzaddikim,* refused to make a vessel and consequently starved to death.[83]

There is a conclusion however that can be calculated. A Jew fulfilling his purpose will be looked after by *Hashem;* the more genuine time he spends on this purpose, the lesser the vessel of work required. The more he ignores his function in the world, the greater must the vessel be.

What then of this section of Talmud at the beginning of this chapter? If a person says, "I strived and failed" — don't believe him. "I didn't strive and succeeded" — don't believe him. "I strived and succeeded" — believe him. How does this stand in the face of everything we have learned? This section of Talmud clearly suggests that the harder you try, the better is your edge at succeeding. This section of Talmud expresses *spiritual* endeavors.[84] Learning Torah and doing *mitzvos.* Learning Torah and doing *mitzvos* is absolutely directly connected with a man's effort. It is difficult. There are aspects of *Yiddishkeit* which are wonderful. *Chassidus* teaches a man to soar in the heavens and to see with new eyes but there are aspects of learning how and doing so which are very difficult. This is where the head and heart are required. Exertion with the head and heart in Torah and *mitzvos* take a Jew out of the realm of weariness and on to the mountain top of fulfillment. There — if a man strives and succeeds — believe him.

---

82. See *Shabbos* 33b.
83. See *Berachos* 35b.
84. See *Megillah* 6b.

LIFE SECRETS — CHAPTER 3

AHAVAS YISRAEL
LOVE YOUR FELLOW JEW
LIKE YOURSELF
CAN IT *REALLY* BE DONE?

We are commanded to love our neighbor (fellow Jew) as oneself.[85] Who can do this? It may be possible to tolerate or like a stranger, but a bothersome neighbor whose faults are patently obvious? How can it be done?

The *mitzvah* of *ahavas Yisrael* is the *mitzvah* which hastens the coming of Moshiach.[86]

The First *Bais HaMikdash* (Temple) lasted for 410 years and was destroyed because of idol worship. Jews were expelled from Israel and experienced a relatively short *golus* (exile) in Babylonia. 72 years later, Ezra returned[87] with them to Israel and built the Second *Bais HaMikdash* which lasted 420 years, and was destroyed by the sin of causeless hatred.[88] The second destruction has left us in this *golus* for over two thousand years. Idol worship caused *golus* for 70 years and the sin of hating other Jews for no reason has caused a *golus* for two thousand years. Clearly therefore the sin of hating a fellow Jew is greater in a sense than idol worship. The Rebbe has explained that Moshiach will be brought by the opposite of this sin, causeless love, which is the *mitzvah* of *ahavas Yisrael*.

Not only must there be causeless love but also the love for the other must be the same as the love one has for oneself.

---

85. See *Leviticus* 19:18.
86. See for example *Likkutei Sichos*, Vol. 23, p. 311; Vol. 13, p. 291.
87. See *Ezra* Chapter 1.
88. See *Yoma* 96b.

This is a very difficult requirement for most of us are not naturally so forgiving of a space-taking associate whose faults glare like beacons.

There is a key to understanding how to do it. We will learn the *chochmah* and *binah* (see Building Block No. 3) together, which are great secrets. The *daas* must come from each man trying to climb the mountain of *Chassidus*. It is difficult. We go a step at a time and, as the fingernails tear from the climb, remember the view from the top...

We have learned that every *neshomah* (divine soul) has its *yeridah* (descent) into its body in order to refine the body by overcoming the *Nefesh HaBahamis* and elevate the environment in order to make a dwelling place for *Hashem* in the lowest of all possible worlds, the physical world.[89] We have also learned that *neshomos* are given a perfect arena to achieve their purpose in life. If a *neshomah's* purpose in life is to give charity, money may be plentiful; if to overcome lusts he may be given bountiful opportunities to exercise control. It bears repeating that living out one's purpose has as its by-products fulfillment, satisfaction and indeed happiness. Ignoring one's purpose puts one in the position of always seeming to be bumping into doors.

There is however a negative side to this in that every *neshomah* has certain areas of vulnerability. The *neshomah* is vulnerable because it is necessary for that *neshomah* to have the capacity to be tempted in a certain area or to have exposure to failure in a certain area.

Conversely, every *neshomah* has its strengths; every person will know where he is on more solid ground than his neighbor, whether in kindness, integrity, strength or intellectual ability, etc. Every *neshomah* has a positive high watermark upon which that *neshomah* can rely.

It now becomes clear why Torah forbids judging a man until one is in his place.[90] What does "in his place" mean? Simply, the

---

89. See *Tanya,* Chapter 33.
90. See *Ethics of Our Fathers* 2:4.

same circumstances as those of the other individual. At a deeper level however we can understand that, even if Shimon's physical place is similar to that of Reuven, this says nothing of his spiritual position. Unless it is in the same spiritual position, how can one *neshomah* possibly judge another?![91]

A wider point is that one *neshomah*'s mission in life is not the same as somebody else's mission in life. Again, therefore, how can they compare? So why then is one's neighbor failing when we are not failing? Because his *neshomah* is vulnerable in a specific area and our *neshomah* is not vulnerable in that specific area.[92] Success is only an achievement for the *neshomah* with the difficulty. There is nothing remarkable about being able to walk; but it is an achievement for a lame man to walk. For a man who is not lame to compare his walking to a man on crutches is not only inappropriate, it is foolish.

We criticize another man because we make a judgmental decision about that person's inability to function in comparison to our ability to function in a given situation. This is an unjustified judgmental decision because it assumes the other person has the same givens. It is just as unfair as demanding of a six year old to lift a suitcase because it is not heavy for an adult.

So a fundamental problem with people's inability to deal with one another's failings is that they measure those failings against their own strengths. This is absolutely forbidden and unjustifiable. If a man observes a weakness in his neighbor in, for example, the neighbor's propensity to gossip, he cannot measure this against his own lack of interest in gossip — because that is not his weakness. He may have a weakness with lust. If he were to compare at all, and we have seen this is idiotic, it should at least be a comparison between the neighbor's gossip and his lust. Ultimately however the only Judge can be *Hashem* because only He knows with what strengths and weaknesses each *neshomah* began.

The above will assist understanding the concepts of causeless hatred and its obverse, causeless love. Normally, healthy

---

91. See *Tanya,* Chapter 30.
92. See also *Ethics of Our Fathers* 1:6.

psychologically sound people concentrate on the positives in themselves. They congratulate themselves on their abilities and successes and make a point of overlooking their shortcomings. Indeed, they justify and rationalize their shortcomings. The requirement of the *mitzvah* of *ahavas Yisrael* is that a man function in the same way with other people. This is to love another person like oneself. Like oneself means to spend no time on their faults and to spend a lot of time on their positives. How does one spend no time on their faults? By understanding that the matters which are unappealing and unattractive about them exist because of a weakness in their *neshomah* which we do not share. If we shared it, we may not do any better and may do much worse.

There is a story about a Rebbe who had a very rich *Chosid* who lived in a very beautiful home. Whenever the Rebbe traveled to the town of the *Chosid*, it was expected that the Rebbe would stay in the *Chosid's* mansion. Whenever the Rebbe arrived into this town however the *Chosid* was away on business with the house closed up. One year the Rebbe arrived unannounced and requested to stay over Shabbos. Over Shabbos, the *Chosid* confessed to his Rebbe that he had always been away deliberately on previous visits. He expected the Chassidim, who would crowd to see the Rebbe, to trek mud and dirt on his beautiful white carpet and white sofas. The Rebbe told him an extraordinary story. Apparently, once there was a man who died, and, when he reached the gates of *Gan Eden,* it was judged that his transgressions outweighed his merits. Before judgment was passed, his defending counsel pointed out that once he saved a family's life. This was put on the balance but it was not enough. His counsel reminded the court that he had saved all the family's possessions and they were thus able to marry off three generations of daughters. The scales were now even. Finally, the angel argued that when he saved the family, they trekked mud and filth onto, and ruined, his only wagon. This tipped the balance. Counsel for the prosecution argued that mud and dirt should not count because that was not part of the *mitzvah*. The defense attorney pressed the recognition of the dirt. Mud and dirt on the scale, off the scale, on the scale. Judgment could not be resolved until, finally, it was decided that that *neshomah* must descend again, its sole test to be the issue of dirt....

His neighbors could not judge the *Chosid* for loving his white carpet and sofas because they could never know the givens of his *neshomah*. If the weakness in his *neshomah* is specifically for white carpet and sofas, then when he has learned to tolerate their use by sincere Jews needing to see their Rebbe, he is springboarded to *Gan Eden*.

The Talmud explains that when we are confronted with a person's[93] fault, we see a mirror image of our own problem. Shimon may for example be sitting at a table with Reuven who is obsessed by dishonesty. Reuven believes everyone steals; the housekeeper steals, the cleaner steals, the employees steal. He has five sets of keys and a combination lock and still they steal. Everyone robs him day and night. Why is Shimon hearing this? Because he Shimon has a problem with stealing. One of the surest tests in *Chassidus* of where one's own negatives are in one's *neshomah*, is to isolate the things most personally troublesome about other people.

So to summarize: We are upset by others in areas we need to remedy in ourselves. However, we cannot judge them because if we had their givens we may well do worse. What we must do is regard them with the same accent on their virtues and blindness to their faults as we do with ourselves. These are the instructions to the *mitzvah* of *ahavas Yisrael*. One can vary the speed and effectiveness of success at performing *mitzvah* of *ahavas Yisrael* by focusing through the lens of what we learned in Building Block No. 4 on space. A man who has trained himself to require little space will not find these instructions as difficult as the man with a swollen *yeshus*. Which comes first? Keeping the instruction or working on oneself? The answer is both; nowhere in this book is there a promise that any of this is easy. There is however a promise that these are gates to Paradise.

---

93.   See *Kiddushin* 77a.

LIFE SECRETS — CHAPTER 4

PLEASURE

Pleasure is a difficult subject to learn with a beginner in *Chassidus*. Most people are brought up with a prejudice that, since pleasure feels good, more must logically be better. People assure us this is so. The media scream it and indeed personal experience, to a limited extent, suggests it.

Loosely put, the argument is that providing one is not hurting another, life's goal is to maximize physical pleasures, whether they are food, drink or sexual relations. Barely post-teenage writers in the advertising industry advise the trusting masses "If it feels good, do it". People who have been slowly conditioned respond with glee. They forget to test the intellect, let alone the wisdom, of the pagan manipulators who create the advertisements.

What happens when we do test the pleasure notion? If the more pleasure the more happiness, are those indulging their pleasures to every conceivable extent happy? Is Hollywood happy? Why do the Elvis Presleys suicide? Ah yes you say. With *my* perspective's and *their capacity* to buy pleasure *I* would be happy. Wrong. If we learn only one thing together with this book, know that pleasure is at best irrelevant to happiness and fulfillment.

This may seem to be disappointing news. It is not. Everyone will grudgingly agree that happiness is much more important than pleasure. They simply do not want to surrender the pleasures in which they indulge, but the path to happiness for a Jew lies in fulfilling his purpose, not in exercising his tastes for ecstasy.

The question that we will address together then is, what is the status of pleasure? How much is a positive? Is it correct to move away from it absolutely or partially, and if so, what is gained? Alternatively, is there a positive in either complete or partial indulgence?

In general terms physical pleasure is the domain of the *Nefesh HaBahamis* and the *yetzer hora* (See Building Block No. 6). The more you feed it the more it grows and the greater is it's consequent appetite.

It is possible to become more expert in every pleasure. Sadly from the perspective of the pleasure seeker, the law of diminishing returns applies. More pleasure is required to do the same job. The level of expertise increases with practice, but the more vigorous the habits the less the return. Furthermore the more frequent the physical pleasure activity, the less room there is for the *Nefesh HoElokis* (See Building Block No. 6).[94]

Conversely, and curiously, the more that pleasure is denied the more the need withers; the more the need is stunted in its growth, the greater the space for growth of the spiritual. This is very important because there is absolutely no comparison between the benefits which flow from the spiritual to those enjoyed at the physical.

The early Chassidim would try to avoid enjoying any physical pleasures. The Alter Rebbe used to say that, that which is forbidden is forbidden without question, but that which is permitted one also does not have to do[95]. Accordingly some Jews throughout history have gone to great lengths not to enjoy anything physical. Some especially wore ill fitting clothes, some ate food they especially disliked. Some over salted the food to diminish the pleasure of tasting it.

This was done by some of the greatest *Rebbeim* of all time, and this chapter does not question their action as correct at the time. In those generations it was obviously correct to do so. The times were of great physical poverty and in those generations the tests were therefore tests of poverty. Today the tests of our generation are different, and are amongst others, tests of wealth.

Since the turn of the century the test of Jews all over the world *Boruch Hashem* seems to be a ridiculously divergent wealth;

---

94. See *Tanya,* Chapter 3 and Chapter 9ff.
95. See *Igros Kodesh of the Previous Rebbe* Vol. 4, p. 74.

ridiculous compared to the socio economic fabric of the rest of humanity. If the number of Jews are considered against the backdrop of world population, the average per capita socio economic position of Jews against the rest of humanity is extraordinarily disproportionate. This is particularly remarkable because no longer can this be attributed to different education standards or isolated living conditions.

It is our generation therefore that is given the job of introducing spirituality into physical plenty.[96] This was not the task of the early Chassidim bereft of anything but the barest essentials.

We elevate that environment by bringing spirituality into physicality and we know that the Rebbe has encouraged use of every form of technological advancement, explaining that the task for Jews is to convert that technological advancement to good.[97] For example, a video can be used to watch negative entertainment or it can be used to watch something which lifts the soul. It is impossible to make a dwelling place in physicality by ignoring physicality.

This being so there appears to be a dilemma; on the one hand we are encouraged to deny excess of comfort and pleasure. Even acknowledging that this allows for more spiritual growth and even supposing a beginner can be satisfied that any self denials are really gates to freedom (as every man on this journey will testify,) still by doing so, one inhibits the opportunity to elevate the very physicality necessary to make a dwelling place for *Hashem* in the physical world. To sit and be a spiritual being twenty-four hours a day may be fine; but then there is no reason for the *neshomah* to descend into a body. The *neshomos* on earth could have remained just as well with the angels in *Gan Eden*.

The whole point of the descent is to overcome a series of difficult tests, which everybody experiences, and to grow from them, in so doing elevating the *neshomah* and refining the environment. (See Building Block No. 2)

---

96. See *Betzeil HaChochmah* p. 14ff.
97. See for example *Sicha* printed in *Shiurim BeSefer HaTanya*.

Accepting then our affluence (compared to the rest of the world), what should be the level of involvement in the comforts and pleasures this may bring? The level of involvement is the critical issue. Let us take the example of food. Is the eating of the food undertaken with a *berochah* and for the constructive purpose of fueling the body to learn Torah and perform *mitzvos* — in which case the natural enjoyment is secondary, or is the eating and the pleasure derived therefrom an end in itself?

Pleasure undertaken for its own sake as we have seen leads nowhere but to disappointment. Furthermore it is destructive to spiritual progress. Rejection of pleasure on the other hand, although this will be an effective way of enhancing spiritual progress, is in effect an abdication of the responsibility of our generation. The ideal level is to participate in every pleasure permitted (and obviously this includes those which accompany *mitzvos*) but with a focused perspective.

This perspective involves an appreciation of the plenty being enjoyed. It acknowledges the fact that, although there were people who would reject such plenty, in this generation there exists the capacity not to reject but to infuse it with spirituality. The involvement must be with the infusion; not the pleasure itself.

The power to infuse physicality with spirituality has become increasingly available in our times. This is the reason why the early Chassidim turned their backs on it. This power is amazingly potent; know that there is a capacity for a Jew to learn *Chassidus*, to learn Torah and to be rich, and yet to be unmoved by that wealth except to recognize a responsibility to give *tzedakah*.

Each of us bless each other for the test of great wealth and the power to overcome being shortchanged by its misuse.

LIFE SECRETS — CHAPTER 5
THE WORLD TO COME

The Torah tells us that if a Jew lives well and fulfills his purpose, his reward is the World to Come. On the other hand, we are told that *all* Jews will inherit the World to Come.[98] This implies even those who have not lived well and fulfilled their purpose. Which is correct?

The Torah is the wisdom of *Hashem*. It follows that it is endlessly deep and infinitely wide. It applies exactly to, and equally in, all times and places and can have no conflicts. Any apparent inconsistency can always be reconciled depending only on the level of our appreciation.

The Rebbe has explained[99] that *Olam Habo* (the World to Come) is a term which refers to two separate states.

The first is *Gan Eden*. It is the state of *neshomos*, when they have successfully finished their *mitzvos*, refining the various bodies in which they have been enclothed and elevating their environment. The *neshomah* is in *Gan Eden* as a reward. There it learns the Torah it learned on earth at a much higher level, and basks in the glow of *Hashem's* presence.

We are told that this is so pleasurable that one moment of this pleasure is more than the entire life on this world.[100]

The other state of the World to Come, is *Techias HaMeisim* (the Revival of the Dead). This will be a time when *neshomos* are resurrected into the bodies that were their attire, so being brought

---

98. See *Sanhedrin* beginning of the Chapter *Cheilek*.
99. For the following explanation see *Sefer HaMaamarim Melukot* Vol. 4, p. 177ff (translated by Sichos in English In *Anticipating the Redemption p.* 40ff).
100. See *Ethics of Our Fathers* 4:17.

back to life. The period of *Techias HaMeisim* will follow the revelation of Moshiach.[101]

The Rebbe has explained that those people who are alive when Moshiach comes will not necessarily die before the period of *Techias HaMeisim*.

So the contradiction is resolved; *Gan Eden* is reward for some; *Techias HaMeisim* rewards all Jews. Both are the World to Come.

What happens to *neshomos* who do not merit *Gan Eden?* They have Gehinom. The word merit is not used in the sense of a naughty child being rapped over the knuckles. The notion is that the *neshomah* has not been elevated to the point where it warrants *Gan Eden*. Those who cannot pass into *Gan Eden* withdraw to Gehinom. There, *neshomos*, stained with their transgressions, are scrubbed spotless. As a facet of *Hashem's* kindness, they are then able to move on to *Gan Eden* or their next *Gilgul* (life cycle).

Which is higher? *Gan Eden* or *Techias HaMeisim?* The answer to, and the understanding of, this question is the fascinating logical conclusion of all *Chassidus*. It is a secret so little understood that many fine scholars could never have navigated these waters of Torah without the beacon of *Chassidus*.

First, the Rebbe explains, *Techias HaMeisim* is later in time. As a culmination of everything, it must be a higher level.[102] But is that not strange? On the one hand, Jews who have lived exemplary lives are rewarded with *Gan Eden*. On the other hand, the whole rabble of Jewry, who ignore our laws, steal, commit commercial rape and pillage and think of only themselves, are sharing *Techias HaMeisim* with *Tzaddikim!* How can that be?

The world is divided into Torah and *mitzvos*. Torah is the spiritual, *mitzvos* is the physical. The physical follows the spiritual. There is a story of a Rebbe who was alive at the time America was first mapped out. When he was brought a map of America, he examined it and pronounced it to be incorrect. There was skepticism from some of those who should have known better.

---

101. See the 13 Principles of facts of the *Rambam*.
102. See *Rambam* at the end of *Shaar HaGammul; Likkutei Torah*, Tzav 15c.

When it was in fact found that the map was wrong, one of the Chassidim asked the Rebbe how he knew. The Rebbe replied that he looked into the letter Beis of the first word of the Torah, Bereishis, and that is how he knew. What does that mean? For a Rebbe, a *Tzaddik,* who knows spirituality, the physical follows naturally.

So what does it mean the world is divided into Torah and *mitzvos?* It means the spiritual and the physical, the *neshomah* and the body, a driving force and an activity. Because there is Torah and *mitzvos*, there is a *neshomah* and a body. There is a spiritual force, the Torah, and the physical activity, the *mitzvos*.

Then comes the question: which is higher — Torah or *mitzvos?* the spiritual or the physical?

In the revealed sense Torah is higher than *mitzvos* because *mitzvos* are spawned from Torah. But ultimately that is not so. The whole purpose of Torah is the *mitzvos*. So, the *mitzvos* are really the main thing.

Although at first glance it appears that a Jew taking somebody across the road or refraining from stealing from him or overcoming his natural urge to put in a false insurance claim does not compare with the difficulties of learning the infinite concepts of Torah, yet this is not so. The whole of the Torah he has learned is only to instruct him to do those things. The whole learning is ultimately for action.

So the main thing is the ultimate result. Consider the example of baking a cake; when the baker thinks of his cake, what he thinks of first is the ultimate result, the ultimate cake, with its chocolate icing, the cherry on top. The purpose of the recipe and the ingredients all lead to the result of the finished cake.

If the purpose of Torah is the doing of the *mitzvos*, which then is higher the *neshomah* or the body? This is an incredible question; the knee jerk reaction is of course the *neshomah* because the *neshomah* is spiritual. However, the reverse is true; the whole purpose of the *neshomah* is only to enliven the body to action.

We have learned that the reward of *Gan Eden* is for the *neshomah*. The spirit benefits because of its completeness and can then be exposed to a revelation of G-dliness. It is pleasurable beyond imagination, but it is not the ultimate level. The ultimate level must be the body level — the ultimate purpose level. That level is *Techias HaMeisim*.

Every Jew is as full of *mitzvos* as a pomegranate with seeds.[103] Even our law-ignoring-thief, mentioned earlier, cumulatively through all his journeys through his various life cycles, is now as full of *mitzvos* as a pomegranate.

Mitzvos are recognized at *Techias HaMeisim*. Learning Torah is recognized at *Gan Eden*. As the main thing is the body *(mitzvos)*, the main thing is *Techias HaMeisim*. *Techias HaMeisim* comes after *Gan Eden* because it is its completion. All Jews have a portion there because all Jews have *mitzvos*, even though all Jews do not have Torah. So it is that all Jews have a share in the World to Come which is *Techias HaMeisim*.

We are told that the job of doing all *mitzvos* cumulatively through all the life cycles is now complete. Moshiach will be immediately revealed and this final stage of the World to Come will be upon us all.

---

103. See end of *Chagigah* 27a.

PART THREE
SECRETS OF THE FESTIVALS

SECRETS OF THE FESTIVALS
CHAPTER 1

ROSH HASHANAH

A Jewish *Yom Tov* is unlike a secular holiday. For the Queen's Birthday, an arbitrary date is chosen and agreed upon. In Jewish law, there is no accident in the date of a festival. When a *Yom Tov* is celebrated, there is a spiritual difference.[104] At that time, a specific revelation of G-dliness is available into which the Jew can tune. On Pesach, it is the revelation of the *emunah* (faith). On Sukkos, it is *simchah*. Rosh HaShanah has a serious and weighty revelation; that of the initial creation of the world and the revelation of *Malchus* (kingship).[105]

When the Alter Rebbe (the first Rebbe of Lubavitch and the author of the *Tanya*) was imprisoned, his cell was denied light.. It was therefore impossible to distinguish between night and day. Extraordinarily, he demonstrated, that he knew the time whether it was night or day. His jailer asked the Alter Rebbe how he knew. The Alter Rebbe explained that the day was divided into so many units (the Jewish time unit is different — the day hours are broken up into certain time zones) and the Alter Rebbe disclosed to him that each one of those time units has a different level of spiritual light; a different revelation of G-dliness. For him therefore it was not difficult to identify that revelation of G-dliness which corresponded to a particular time[106].

When the Ruziner Rebbe was a little boy his teacher was teaching him the laws of Shabbos. There are laws in relation to what a person should do if he finds himself lost in a desert, unable to identify which day is Shabbos. The young boy told his teacher there

---

104. See for example *Igros Melech* Vol. 1, p. 33b.
105. See *Ibid.,* Vol. 1, p. 39.
106. See *The Arrest and Liberation of Rabbi Schneur Zalman of Liadi,* p. 41.

was no problem as all he had to do was to look up into the sky and see when Shabbos was coming. The teacher, thinking he was being cheeky, smacked him. His father, then Rebbe, found the boy crying and inquired as to what happened. When the boy told him, the Rebbe explained to the teacher gently to leave the boy — his son could in fact see when Shabbos was coming.

Men of great spiritual stature have the capacity to receive this revelation daily. On the festivals however even the average Jew is affected by the revelation of G-dliness which radiates on that festival. On Rosh HaShanah every Jewish *neshomah* can tune in to the level of G-dliness being revealed that day. Many Chassidic stories witness that special skills are unnecessary.

In the shul of The Baal Shem Tov in Europe, a boy entered the synagogue on Rosh HaShanah and, being ignorant of the prayers, just kept saying the *Alef-Beis* at the front of the Siddur. He was observed crying and laughing and from time to time clapping much to the consternation of the serious congregation. After Rosh HaShanah concluded, the Rebbe announced that the Jewish world in Russia that year was saved because of this boy. The boy had told *Hashem* that he did not know how to daven, that he did not know how to learn, but that he knew the *Alef-Beis*. He resolved to spend all day saying the letters and asked *Hashem* to rearrange them. His davening was accepted as the best davening for the whole of Jewry Rosh HaShanah that year. This is the level of sincerity every Jew can achieve. Every Jew can tune into the revelation of G-dliness on Rosh HaShanah at his level.

Rosh HaShanah is the day which celebrates the creation of the world; not the first but the sixth day. The world was created on the 25th of Elul,[107] six days before the end of the month before. The sixth day of creation, 1st of Tishrei, is Rosh HaShanah, the day on which humanity was created.

We regard this day as the birthday of the world.[108] This means that *Hashem's* creative process culminated physically on Rosh HaShanah in the creation of humanity. Every Rosh HaShanah that

---

107. See *Vayikra Rabbah,* Chapter 29.
108. See *Mussaf Prayer on Rosh HaShanah — HaYom Haros Olom.*

process is being re-enacted for the following year. Exactly the same spiritual forces involved in creating the world, re-happen Rosh HaShanah. We are able to tune into that process and we will learn about that spiritual force together.

Every child knows that Rosh HaShanah is the Day of Judgment.[109] A moment's examination of a decently translated *Machzor* will evidence that it is replete with the whole notion of the Day of Judgment for the whole world for the ensuing year. To be determined is who will live and who will die, who will be rich and who will be poor, who will be healthy and who will be sick, who will be barren and who will be fruitful, who will be insane and who will be mentally healthy.

Curiously however there is a *Gemora* which says that *Hashem* judges us every day,[110] indeed every moment. How can both things be true? Is it Judgment for the year, for the day or for the moment? Does that Judgment take place Rosh HaShanah or daily?

Everything physical is a product of something spiritual. All physical matter is a precipitation of its spiritual source. On Rosh HaShanah a spiritual potential is created. Subsequently, there is a process of drawing down that spiritual potential by condensing it into something physical. If a man does not behave as he should or changes direction in some way, the drawing down and condensation of that spirituality into physicality may be frustrated. Conversely, a change for better may increase the conduit for drawing down potential blessing.[111]

An example of a spiritual force in potential becoming actual is set out in the Talmud: Rabbi Akiva, one of the outstanding personalities of the *Gemora*, had a daughter who was married at a great wedding in the presence of all the Torah sages of the generation. Upon her birth Astrologers predicted she would die on the night of her wedding. On the night of her wedding, she took her hat pin and inserted it into a hole in the wall, the then customary place for their storage. In the morning a death adder was discovered

---

109. See *ibid., the prayer of Unesaneh Tokef.*
110. See *Rosh HaShanah* 16a.
111. See *Sefer HaMaamarim Melukot* Vol. 4, p. 291.

hanging on the other end of the hat pin, pierced through the brain. She told her father who then inquired as to her actions on the night of her wedding. It should be explained that religious weddings provide a table for the poor where anyone deprived may come and eat. She then explained to her father that on that night the poor people were at their table ignored by everyone. Indeed, no-one was serving them food and they were apparently embarrassed to ask. The bride left her dancing, served their food and cleaned up after them personally. Rabbi Akiva then explained this great secret of Torah. Her activity interfered with that spiritual force even as it was being actualized. Her hat pin wielded by her merit lanced the snake which was the actualized result of this spiritual force.

The spiritual potential for all human condition is created Rosh HaShanah. So it was the first Rosh HaShanah on the sixth day of creation.

But here is the secret. That potential to become a physical actuality can be and is in fact interfered with by Jews. In fact, the capacity to interfered with that spiritual force is absolutely unrestricted. A Jew, though *teshuvah*,[112] can change any decree against other Jews serially and generally. Purim is a good example. Jews were decreed, G-d forbid, to be annihilated that year. Jews did *teshuvah* and the decree was abrogated. This principle is so important it bears restating. The destiny of the world, the blessings and the reverse decreed on Rosh HaShanah by *Hashem* can be affected by Jewish behavior.

As we have by now learned, the purpose of the descent of a *neshomah* into the body is to learn Torah and do *mitzvos*. More specifically, the work of the *neshomah* is to elevate its body and to refine its environment. A man needs to neutralize his *Yetzer Hora* and refine his physical environs. This is how Jews bring G-dliness into the world and this is a sacred task. Before the sixth day, there was no man. Before there was man, there was no need for revealed G-dliness and there was no pathway to bring it down. So what we are doing Rosh HaShanah is enormously important because it is the

---

112. See end of *Unesaneh Tokef prayer*, *"and Teshuvah, Tefillah and Tzedakah change the bad decree"*.

day on which the whole rest of the year's spiritual potential is mapped out and how we Jews behave as a nation on Rosh HaShanah is absolutely connected to how the rest of the year develops.[113] If Jews are good, we have rain and we have prosperity. If Jews are not good, if Jews fight, slander, steal and shame each other, if their *yetzer hora* is, G-d forbid, triumphant, then we have bad years. It is an extraordinary exercise to view world history through the lens of Jewish behavior. The times of exploration, expansion and success and the times of darkness and geographic misery are directly attributable to Jewish *avodah* (service). If the *avodah* is strong, we have progressive years for everybody.

---

113. See for example *Igros Kodesh of the Previous Rebbe* Vol. 6, p. 429 with regard to our conduct on Rosh HaShanah.

SECRETS OF THE FESTIVALS
CHAPTER 2

YOM KIPPUR

Yom Kippur is the day of *teshuvah* for all Jews.[114] *Teshuvah* in Hebrew does not mean repentance as is usually mistranslated and as we understand it in English. *Teshuvah* really means return. The word in Hebrew connotes a return along the same road.[115]

On Yom Kippur it is a *mitzvah* for every Jew to do *teshuvah* and every Jew includes *Tzaddikim*.[116] What does it mean for a Rebbe, a *Tzaddik,* with no *Yetzer Hora* with no difficulty in overcoming the tests of ordinary people in this world, to do *teshuvah*? It cannot simply be a regret for sin; if that were so, *Tzaddikim* would have no job to do on Yom Kippur. The answer is that *teshuvah* connotes the return to the connection to *Hashem* at such level that existed before the descent of the *neshomah* into the body.[117] A *Tzaddik* has the capacity to return to his source, i.e. his *neshomah* to *Hashem's* essence as does a lowly transgressor. At this level, the *neshomah* is free of transgressions, free from any non-observance of *mitzvos*. This is the background to the dynamics of *neshomos* on Yom Kippur.

Jews exist on this planet because their *neshomos* are reluctantly lowered down into bodies, unwilling occupiers of a hostile environment. The task of each *neshomah* is to overcome the newfound needs and lusts of the physical body in a physical environment. It is not sufficient to describe the *neshomah's* return to its source; we need to conceive as far as possible what that source is.

---

114. See *Rambam, Laws of Teshuvah* 2:7.
115. See *Likkutei Sichos,* Vol. 2, p. 409.
116 *Ibid.*
117. See *Likkutei Sichos,* Vol. 20, p. 273ff.

Hashem created the first man and blew into his nostrils a breath of life.[118] Blowing is a much deeper level than speaking. When a person speaks, he speaks basically with his mouth, tongue, lips, teeth and larynx. When he blows, the breath comes from the most innermost part of the person. A person can talk all day with little likelihood of being tired. Should he however attend his nine year old's birthday party and be assigned the job of inflating fifty balloons, he will probably experience exhaustion.

It is fascinating that one of the great secrets of Torah is that the whole order of creation was done through ten sayings. G-d said, "Let there be light", "Let there be heaven", "Let there be an earth", "Let there be lights in the sky", etc. The creative process was by speech. Speech is an outer garment and sets up a reflection of a reflection of a reflection, until the reflection becomes so faint that ultimately we have nature which is a shield of, and an impediment to, seeing G-dliness.

The *neshomah* of man, *adom,* on the other hand, was not created by speech but by G-d blowing, so to speak, from His inside. All previous creation was from *Hashem's* speech, so to speak, from His more external level.

We have learned (see Building Block No. 2) that there is no descent without the potential for a corresponding ascent. The reluctant *neshomah* undergoes the enormous descent, from the highest level of being one with *Hashem* to the lowest level of inhabiting a physical body in a physical world. The purpose of this exile to a hostile environment is to ultimately ascend to a level higher than before the descent.[119] This principle holds true of all human endeavor whether spiritual, intellectual or physical.

Sometimes the *neshomah* will fail to be elevated through failing the tests which are of course opportunities for this elevation. A moments reflection sees these tests falling into three categories: —

The first is the category of overcoming one's needs. Every *neshomah* battles to both satisfy and overcome the needs and lusts

---

118. See *Lessons In Tanya,* Vol. I, Chapter 2.
119. See *Torah Or, Noach* 58d.

of the body. The constant temptation is to overindulge even in things permitted. The cravings of our flesh are orchestrated into symphonies of persuasion by the intellect.

The second is the category of coping with the environment. The physical problems of heat, cold and shelter, and gaining sufficient income appear to be a full time job.

The third is the category of trying to keep in perspective daily that one is a *neshomah* in a body and that all that is going on physically is only a series of tests. Jews are not sent down into this world with the sole purpose of accumulating $10m. We are here for a specific task; to refine the body and to elevate the environment.

The job is so difficult because the descent is so great. We can all testify that it is enormously difficult not only monthly or weekly but daily; not only daily but hourly and momentarily. The failure rate seems great and the penalty for that failure rate is the progressive severance of the *neshomah* from its source. At a conscious level any such severance would be unthinkable for a Jew as there is a natural dependence of every *neshomah* upon *Hashem*. If he only knew about it at the time, whenever a Jew commits a transgression, there is a disconnection of that relationship. He goes momentarily blind and experiences amnesia.[120] Forgotten is *Hashem,* forgotten is the plight of the *neshomah*, all reality is restricted to the object of the momentary desire. On Yom Kippur the process of *teshuvah* is to make good all the single acts of severance between a *neshomah* and *Hashem* that took place all year long, to return the *neshomah* to that "place" from which it was blown.

As we will learn together in the chapter on Purim, there is in the world that which we see as nature, and there is that which is above nature.[121] Jews are connected to that which is above nature. The nations of the world are entrusted to study nature. Their task is immensely important; we need the fruits of this study and we learn from, and use, the resultant technology. Nevertheless, the nations are studying the curtain and our function is to be in touch with what is behind the curtain. We, are entrusted with the task of

---

120. See *Sefer HaMaamarim Basi LeGani,* p. 4.
121. See *Likkutei Sichos,* Vol. 1, p. 213ff.

bringing that which is behind the curtain into view and existence in physicality.

A physical example is fire. Scientists define fire in various ways. The most common definition is light and heat coupled with combustion. The nations have brought about amazing discoveries proceeding from this observation of strands of the curtain. This definition is fine for studying the curtain. Behind the curtain we learn that fire is one of the four *yesoidos* (foundations) of creation.[122] For fire to exist on a candle, there must be a wick. At a spiritual level, the wick of G-dliness in this world is Torah and *mitzvos*.[123] A Jew doing 248 positive *mitzvos* and 365 negative *mitzvos* keeps the spiritual flame on the physical wick, the wick of *mitzvos*. If there were no wick, G-d forbid, the flame of spiritual light would disappear from the physicality. Consequently, it is revealed in Torah that unless there are Jews learning Torah and doing *mitzvos* the world will vanish.[124] Why? Because there will be no wick. There must be a wick however small.

In order for there to be a choice, it needs to be equal.[125] Not only equal, but exactly equal. So equal that the choice is absolute. This means that if there is a positive priority to go right, there must be a negative availability to go left of exactly the same intensity. Otherwise, there is no choice. So if we are going to have a fire in the world and if that fire is going to have the wick of *mitzvos*, and that is the fire of G-dliness, there must be an equal fire, that is a strange fire, and there has to be *kelipah*[126] (evil) — and the wick for *kelipah* is thought, speech and action of a negative kind.

Consider stealing:

A person is financially pressured. His kids need braces on their teeth. Let us forget about having needs that are physical dependencies. Everybody knows what financial pressures are from time to time. There is the apparent alternative of stealing some

---

122. See *Rambam, Hilchos Yesodei HaTorah* 3:10.
123. See *Proverbs* 6:23.
124. See *Pesachim* 68b.
125. See for example *Likkutei Sichos*, Vol. 20, p. 108.
126. See *Likkutei Torah, Bamidbar* 94a.

money or manipulating money by way of some kind of theft. The thought, speech and action of that process is the wick for that strange fire. It is the greatest stupidity because, if a man really believes in G-d and *Hashgochah Protis*; if he understands that, subject only to his effort, his portion is handed out on Rosh HaShanah, imagining that he can take the portion of somebody else when *Hashem* is not looking is totally childish because it exhibits lack of *daas* (See Building Block No. 3).

On Yom Kippur, one has to fan out all the strange fire and dismantle those wicks. Repentance is also commendable. The issue however is that one has got to scramble back to above the position from which he moved into wrong. This may be difficult because, in the case of our thief, he has to first make restitution of the money. On Yom Kippur, we seek forgiveness for two distinct categories of transgressions. There are those a person does man to man and there are those a person does man to G-d. If five days in the year Shimon did not daven *Shema* (it is a *mitzvah* in Torah to daven *Shema* twice a day), then on Yom Kippur he can come to *Hashem* and, if he is sincere and regrets it, he can return his *neshomah* to the position where it was before he neglected to daven *Shema*. But if Shimon has manipulated a theft from Reuven, then he must first restore Reuven's position; only then is a dialogue with *Hashem* available in relation to Reuven.

We are told that a *Baal Teshuvah* stands in a place a *Tzaddik* cannot stand.[127] There are two questions to this; how and why.[128] The how is to make a new wick and relight the extinguished fire. All that is needed is sufficient sincerity. Sufficient *teshuvah* can light the fire with an explosion of cataclysmic proportions. The why lies in the essential difference between a *Tzaddik* and us. A *Tzaddik* has no *Yetzer Hora* left, no desire to do any bad. He is as free from temptations to transgress the will of *Hashem* as a non-smoker is free of the need to smoke a cigarette. Indeed, a complete *Tzaddik* is a vehicle driven entirely by the will of *Hashem*. But when a *Baal Teshuvah* returns his *neshomah* to be reunited with its source —

---

127. See *Talmud Berachos* 34b.
128. See *Likkutei Sichos,* Vol. 20, p. 273 onwards.

which we have learned is part of G-d Himself — the spiritual power released makes a nuclear reaction trivial. All the bad the person has done; all the transgressions are snapped back into *mitzvos* launching the *neshomah* to the highest of peaks. This is the awesome power of a Jew on Yom Kippur. He has the capacity of springboarding his *neshomah* all the way back to its source — all the way back to the essence of *Hashem* Himself. It is the music of this possibility every Jewish *neshomah* hears as Yom Kippur approaches. It is the need to hear this music that magically draws so many Jews to synagogue once a year.

SECRETS OF THE FESTIVALS
CHAPTER 3
SUCCOS

Succos is a festival of paradoxes for the uninitiated. On the one hand, it is accompanied by what seems, G-d forbid, to be strange rites; living by choice in a funny shack, waving various articles of garden produce in fervent rapture and shuffling around the synagogue to repetitive chants. On the other hand, all Jewish children will testify to the fact that Succos is our sweetest festival; a time of joy and song, a little strong drink and much dancing. Most importantly, it is the time of year when Jews concentrate hard on the business of really loving each other and bring that intellectual effort into emotional reality.

What then is really going on? What are the spiritual cloud formations we can, with training, look up and see? The answers go to the deepest and most exciting levels of Torah.

We will see together when learning about Shavuos that *Hashem* changed creation at the time of the giving of the Torah on Mount Sinai.[129] From then on, *neshomos* were able to effect a crossing from the spiritual to the physical. It is sufficient here to note this and to understand perhaps later that Jews actually have the power to infuse the physical with the spiritual. It is of course this wondrous power which gives Jews the ability to make a dwelling place for *Hashem* in the lowest of possible worlds — this one, which is, after all, the whole purpose of physical creation.

We begin with the *mitzvah* to live in a *succah* for seven days to remind us that *Hashem* brought us out of *Mitzrayim* in *succos* (i.e.

---

129. See for example *Likkutei Sichos*, Vol. 1, p. 41.

clouds of glory).[130] The knowledge that *Hashem* put us in *succos* is actually part of the *mitzvah*.[131]

How important is the *succah* to a Jew with education? Being the only *mitzvah* a Jew can actually enter and have surround him, its preciousness is incalculable. Chassidim tell a famous story at the time of Succos.[132]

One of Europe's most famous early Chassidic Rebbes, Rabbi Levi Yitzchok was the Rav of Berditchev where one year there was no *esrog*. A visitor was passing through the town. It having come to the attention of R. Levi that the visitor possessed a precious *esrog*, he was summoned to see the Rebbe and invited to stay over Succos. This being impossible for the visitor, R. Levi, in apparent desperation, made him an offer no sane man could refuse. If he stayed in Berditchev that Succos, the *Tzaddik*, by a legally effective process guaranteed to be together with him in the World to Come! The visitor, trembling at the enormity of his good fortune, of course agreed. With his now bankable future, the Jew headed off to synagogue on the first night of the festival, his heart aflame.

Meanwhile the Rebbe secretly had all the townsfolk severely instructed not to allow the visitor into any of their succos under any circumstances whatsoever.

At the conclusion of davening, the stranger waited for the line of people to invite him home — after all, his was now a unique status. As one by one the sturdy folk avoided him, he was forced to be more forthright and began to ask for hospitality. To his dismay, everyone was full up, all with no room for even one more guest.

The stranger began to panic and ran to the Rebbe's *succah* only to be denied admission there too. After desperate inquiry as to what was happening, the Rebbe calmly informed him that he would only be permitted access to the *succah* on reassignment of the promise! The visitor was devastated. How could he, seeing, as it were, into *Gan Eden*, surrender such a prize? Equally, however, how could he be without the *mitzvah* of *succah?!* With tears of frustration and the

130. See *Shulchan Aruch HaRav* 625:1.
131. See commentary of *Bach* on *Ibid*.
132. See *Sippurei Chassidim on Festivals* Vol. 1, p. 117.

demeanor of one totally outmaneuvered, he chokingly returned the trophy. After *Yom Tov* the Rebbe informed the Jew that, because of his choosing the *mitzvah* over even being guaranteed a place with the Rebbe in the World to Come, he had earned a portion of his own there greater than he had surrendered. Such is the power of the *mitzvah* of *Succah*.

The astute reader will have noted from the story not only the importance of the *succah* but also the obvious importance of having the *Esrog*. Equally important are the remaining of the four species of *Lulav, Hadassim* and *Arovos*.

Throughout the festival of Succos, we grasp the four species together and intermittently shake them and draw them to our hearts. Wonderful symbolism exists here; the four species represent four species of *neshomos* within the mighty genus of Jewry.[133]

The *Esrog*	—	a beautiful fruit which has both taste and smell represents the Jew who has both Torah and *mitzvos*.
The *Lulav*	—	a date palm branch has taste but no smell represents the Jew with Torah but lacking in *mitzvos*.
The *Hadassim*	—	myrtle leaves have smell but no taste and represent the Jew with *mitzvos* but no learning.
The *Arovos*	—	willow leaves with neither smell nor taste represent the Jew without either Torah or *mitzvos*.

All too often in the year, the nation of Israel is divided. Succos time, however, all kinds of Jew bind together in pursuit of unity to do *Hashem's* will.

At a much deeper level, it is time to consider another very important set of currents in Torah. Just as we have previously seen the ebb and flow of *golus* and *geulah*; flight and return; descent and ascent — it is time to see the process of *makkif* (encompassing) and

---

133. See *Vayikra Rabbah* 30:12.

pnimiyus (internalizing). Through Torah there are fascinating waves of notions which are makkif which roll towards the beach of a person's endeavors. A *neshomah* induces these waves to break and so internalizes the foam into *pnimiyus* (internal).

A clear example of this is the difference between every Jew's *emunah* (belief and connection with G-d) and his daily understanding of this. His *emunah* is *makkif* (general and encompassing). His understanding is *pnimiyus* (personal to him and internalized). Every Jew from birth by definition, as we have seen earlier, has *emunah* (*makkif* — encompassing). It takes rigorous education however to bring this into personal understanding (*pnimiyus* — internalized).[134]

Marvelously, this same process is available to every Jew daily. He wakes in the morning shaded by the encompassing shelter of his belief in G-d. This however is general and can only be applied to practical use through bringing this general level down to *pnimiyus* (internal) by learning and davening first thing in the morning and then holding that particularization throughout the pulls and pushes of the physical day.

A curious phenomenon occurs when a Jew brings down *makkif* (encompassing) into *pnimiyus* (internal); the power of the level that was *makkif* (encompassing) becomes greater when brought into *pnimiyus* (internal)!

When a Jew learns and daven's (as we have seen bringing down the *emunah* (*makkif* — encompassing) to the *pnimiyus* (internal)), he actually increases the *emunah* and the more it permeates his entire being.

This of course is the tragic mistake of the Jew who asks for a sign before he will act. It is the very action which increases that which is escaping him. Without bringing down the *makkif* (encompassing) to *pnimiyus* (internal), he prevents the growth of the *makkif* (encompassing).

---

134. See for example *Likkutei Sichos*, Vol. 24, p. 182ff.

Rosh HaShanah is *makkif* (encompassing), Yom Kippur *pnimiyus* (internal).[135]

Succos reveals the entire process of Rosh HaShanah and Yom Kippur.[136] In Succos itself, the *succah* is *makkif* (encompassing), shaking the four species is *pnimiyus* (internal).[137] We build the *succah* (*makkif* — encompassing) and enter it to internalize the joining of all categories of Jew into one unity (*pnimiyus* — internal). This is a process which requires seven days. During these seven days every Jew can also take the four categories in *himself* and join them together in a more unified service of G-d.

This then is why we dwell in a *succah* seven days. We are processing, internalizing, drawing down the cataclysmic forces present at Rosh HaShanah and Yom Kippur into a bonding of all Jews of whatever level into service of *Hashem* for the whole year.

Our Rebbe in the story, R. Levi Yitzchok, of course understood all this. The *neshomah* of the simple visitor was great enough to participate in the process just described. A man who will give up paradise to unify the holy nation of Israel is in fact achieving paradise immediately.

---

135. See *Likkutei Torah, Rosh HaShanah* 58b.
136. *Ibid.,* 54d.
137. See for example *Sefer HaMaamarim Melukot* Vol. 1, p. 175ff.

SECRETS OF THE FESTIVALS
CHAPTER 4

CHANUKAH

Most Jewish children know the story of Chanukah.[138] The Syrian-Greeks conquered the Jews and fixed as their object the destruction of Judaism by seeking to force Jews to eliminate G-dliness from Torah. This destruction was epitomized by the defiling of the Temple. Notwithstanding the efforts of the enemy, one cruse of pure olive oil with the stamp of the High Priest was found and used to relight the *menorah*. A miracle took place and the cruse, which normally burned for one day, lasted for eight days, the time required to make the pure oil necessary to keep the flame alive in the *menorah*.

We remember the miracle as the festival of Chanukah.

Curiously, as we will see, we do not remember it primarily as a festival to celebrate the winning of the war or the regaining of the Temple. We celebrate it to remember this miracle of the oil.

There are a few things to note before we learn about the one cruse of oil. People should understand that the *menorah* was lit with perfect, special, pure super quality oil. But in Jewish law,[139] in such an emergency, there is no reason not to use a lower grade. The *menorah* could still have been lit. Nevertheless, the Jews chose to make no compromise to use the perfect oil leaving the outcome to *Hashem*.

It is as well to understand how a *menorah* works. Olive oil is poured into the seven cups. A wick made of fabric, preferably cotton, is then inserted. Interestingly, oil cannot burn on its own; no amount of heat is sufficient to ignite it. The olive oil is drawn into

---

138. See *Shabbos* 21b.
139. See *Mikroei Kodesh on Chanukah* for discussion on this problem.

the wick, which equally interestingly does not burn on its own. When the wick is engorged with oil, the oil burns, not the wick. Clearly however, the size of the wick is variable. Its size determines how much oil is consumed and so burned. It follows that because a thick wick consumes oil more quickly than a thin wick, the time of burning can be varied accordingly. It further follows that with the knowledge of having only one cruse of oil coupled with the knowledge that it takes eight days to make a new cruse of perfect oil, an option is to use a wick one-eighth of the thickness of a standard wick. The oil will then last eight times as long. The *menorah* was large and so the wick was easily slivered into eight pieces in diameter. Again, the choice was the standard wick and the rest was left to *Hashem*.

According to law,[140] the light from the Chanukah *menorah* is entirely different to any other light; all other candle light is a means to an end, whereas the Chanukah *menorah* is an end in itself. This is because, unlike other light which may be for honor (as in, say, a synagogue) or the actual use of the light (for example, over *Havdalah* after Shabbos), it is forbidden to have use from the light of the Chanukah *menorah*. We are forbidden to gain benefit from the light as such.

Why then do Jews place their Chanukah *menorah* in the window? (The Lubavitcher custom is to put it in a doorway, opposite the *mezuzah*.) The light entails a symbol of publicity — can we say this is of no use? Indeed, some people, intent on doing the *mitzvah* beautifully, will display large blazing lights for the world to see.

Nevertheless, that is not the purpose of the *menorah*. The proof is that in times of danger the *menorah* is lit privately — specifically so that it cannot be seen. This is evidence that the publication is not the sole purpose. There is no purpose other than simply the obligation to light.

When a Jew lights his *menorah* therefore, he is doing so with no motive as to utility. He remembers a miracle which occurred when he performed the *mitzvah* without compromise, with a full

---

140. For the following explanation see *Likkutei Sichos,* Vol. 3, p. 814ff.

and sincere heart abandoning the outcome to *Hashem*. If a Jew testifies to this every time he lights, he has just re-examined a secret blueprint for Jewish life generally.

At a deeper level, the Rebbe points out that there are three aspects of Chanukah. One is the decrees made against us by the Greeks, the second is the self-sacrifice of the Jews and the third is that there were two miracles; the war and the lights.

These three aspects together are one of the secrets of the essential connection between every Jew and G-d. The connection is essential because all three things are completely above reason.

Firstly, the decrees:

Curiously, Greeks and Jews lived with each other harmoniously. Jews, particularly those who were less observant, have blended intellectually and culturally with many societies in history. there is a grudging tolerance and, even at certain times, fascination, one with the other. This was true in all places where Jews lived at the time. Often the host nation was powerful; whether Greece, Rome, Spain, England, France or Central Europe, paradoxically Jews' acceptance by the host environment often occurred simultaneously with anti-Semitism.

Greece at the time was of course the hallmark of culture. Within Greek society, as is true today, there were those Jews who were observant Jews, uncompromising in their *Yiddishkeit,* and there were those who lived trying to melt as completely as possible into cultural surroundings.

The decree of the Greeks did not forbid the learning of Torah; rather, the requirement was for the G-dliness to be removed from Torah. Torah was to be understood as having only a rational base.

Oil, the symbol of light and G-dliness, needed to be defiled. It was the very insistence on the purity of the oil which corresponds to the insistence of the purity of Torah to be maintained in its pristine state.

Secondly, the self-sacrifice:

The fighting of a persuasive cultural environment which seduces a person into accepting it, was highlighted by the self-sacrifice that the Jews had at that time. Their self-sacrifice was their refusal to compromise and obey the decrees choosing instead a dependence on *Hashem* outside logic. This was particularly so because the Jewish non-logical connection with G-d was the very furnace of the fury of the Greeks.

Finally, the third aspect were the miracles. Miracles are higher than, and outside of, reason. The miracles showed the special connection between the Jews and their G-d.

This supra logical connection between Jews and their G-d at a physical level is embodied in the lights. Israel could have used less pure oil and they could have used smaller wicks. But, for life to be perfect for a Jew, the method is to do the *mitzvos* perfectly and then leave it to *Hashem*. This blind faith in G-d is its own conduit for bringing down the blessings.

The miracle that happened expresses the relationship which transcends limitation. The limitation of that one cruse of oil and a standard size wick. This is why, when we celebrate Chanukah, the Sages made the miracle of the light the main focus of our celebration, not the winning of the war.

The whole point of celebrating Chanukah is the celebration of a Jew's supra natural relationship with G-d. If we do *Hashem's* Will, learn Torah and do *mitzvos*, apart from the by-product of living a purposeful happy life, it is possible to achieve everything.

SECRETS OF THE FESTIVALS
CHAPTER 5

PURIM

Before we can understand what happened on Purim we need to understand that when G-d is not revealed we have nature. Nature hides revealed G-dliness.[141]

Because Jews have a *neshomah* which is part of G-d Himself we have an awesome ability; to reach through the curtain of nature to the level where there is revealed

G-dliness. Revealed G-dliness supersedes nature.

An example of this level brought down into the physical world were the miraculous Luchos (the tablets with the Ten Commandments) which Moshe Rabbeinu brought down from Mount Sinai. Unlike the pictures depicting them, the *Luchos* were a pair of cubes. They were made by *Hashem* with the letters engraved through to the other side. There was no front, there was no back. Although the letters were engraved through to the other side, the writing on the rear face was not reversed![142]

The ability for a Jew to tune in to the level of revealed G-dliness is best exemplified in people by regarding a *Tzaddik*. We know, for example, nature has no dominion over a *Tzaddik*. If a *Tzaddik* directs water to flow uphill, it will flow uphill. In the Talmud, there is a discussion between two *Tzaddikim* who considered walking through a wall.[143] Their decision to desist has nothing to do with whether they are able to do so.

---

141. See for example *Likkutei Sichos,* Vol. 20, p. 36.
142. See *Talmud Yerushalmi Shekalim* 6:1.
143. *Ibid.*

The Alter Rebbe, wanting to bless the moon, stopped the boat on which he was imprisoned without physically interfering with it.[144]

On another occasion when he was being conveyed to prison the day before Shabbos, the Alter Rebbe announced that he did not travel past a certain time the day before Shabbos, and requested his escort to stop. The guard's mirth gave way to fear and respect when the coach wheels kept breaking despite replacement, so that the Alter Rebbe should not have to travel.[145]

Tzaddikim are different to other Jews in the level or degree to which they are tuned into G-dliness. If an ordinary person is tuned into G-dliness properly, he too avoids nature's rule over him.

When a Jew serves *Hashem* so that his whole being is totally dedicated to *Hashem* and his whole life is service to Him with everything else an inconvenient interlude, then the inconvenient interludes will bear no dominion over his life.

Purim is about this notion. The story of Purim is well known to most Jews: The wicked Haman convinced powerful Achashverosh, King of all the provinces in which Jews then lived, to pass a decree that all Jews be wiped out on a certain day. The day was chosen by way of lottery. The killing method was very effective; everybody who killed a Jew would be entitled to keep his property. People responded well to this persuasive argument, and all Jews were to be annihilated on that day. The Jews fasted for three days, prayed and did *teshuvah*.

Esther, the niece of the *Tzaddik* of the generation, Mordechai, was the Queen and changed the King's mind so saving the entire nation. She achieved this by her service to G-d; the result being that the King instead killed Haman and his sons, and *Am Yisrael* lived on.

The story of Purim is the story of our being saved miraculously. It was a miracle because the remedy against Haman is totally without logic. If somebody is going to kill you with a date set six

---

144. See *Sefer HaToldos of the Alter Rebbe*
145. See *Beis Rebbi,* Chapter 21.

months in advance, a sensible man leaves town or prepares to fight, meanwhile putting his house into a family trust. Additionally he may try to persuade Government Authorities by the lobby process. To go to synagogue and fast for three days and pray to *Hashem* is an apparently lunatic method of dealing with the threat. Yet this method and only this method worked. Why?

It is a great secret of Torah[146] that when Jews behave as Jews, they are not limited by nature. In nature the result was to be killed. It was above nature for the decree to be overturned, with Haman left swinging from a tree. Behaving as Jews should allow them to reach out and above the limitations of nature and draw down G-d's essence. This is what we celebrate on Purim.

Extraordinarily not once is *Hashem's* name mentioned in the *Megillah*. It is the only document of Torah where this is so. Nevertheless our sages tell us that "King" in the *Megillah* represents *Hashem*,[147] Mordechai is the Jewish nation, and Haman is the *Yetzer Hora*. The *yetzer hora* pleads with the King to kill all Israel but the result was in favor of Mordechai and Jews forever.

On Purim the story of Purim, the *Megillah*, is read in synagogue. The Rebbe explains in great depth a verse from the *Megillah*,[148] "The King woke up". We have said the King is *Hashem;* can it be said that *Hashem* sleeps?

When Jews behave according to the will of G-d, He is, as it were, awake; when we behave to the contrary, *Hashem* is, as it were, asleep. *Hashem* asleep, is a lack of G-dly revelation, and so nature is what we see and relate to. *Hashem* awake means that there is a revelation of G-dliness which we can see and relate to. When Moshe Rabbeinu received the Tablets on Mount Sinai, when all Jews were unified in *Hashem's* will, *Hashem* was therefore, as it were, awake. His present to the Jewish nation, the Ten Commandments, therefore were a level of revealed G-dliness and so the Tablets had no front and no back. The moment the actions of Jews degenerated,

---

146. See *Likkutei Sichos*, Vol. 1, p. 213ff.
147. See *Yalkut Shimoni on the Megillah* 6:1.
148. For the following explanation see *Sefer HaMaamarim Melukot* Vol. 2, p. 265ff. (See also *Sefer HaMaamarim 5710*, p. 1ff).

so returning *Hashem* to sleep, the revelation of G-dliness was removed and the Tablets were broken.

All powers given to human beings come from the soul. A human soul is equipped with various powers, for example, the power to see and the power to hear. The power exists independently of the limb which is the receptacle of that power. So if a person has the power of sight, he has the power of sight independently of the organ that sees, independently of the eye. If he were to, notionally, take out his eye, vision would be interrupted because the instrument was missing. The moment the eye is restored, he will see again. This is so because the *power* to see remains constant but is only available to be revealed by the presence of that instrument.

Similarly, the power to hear. If the ear is filled with wax, sound waves may no longer have access to the ear drum and the person will not hear. But, of course, the power to hear remains unimpaired. Consider however the finest ear without a soul; kill the man but preserve perfect ears. Can he hear? The power is in the soul in a general level and in the ear in a particular level.

A fascinating thing happens to a man's powers when he is asleep. The powers cannot have disappeared because the person is still alive. The particular powers to the limbs however are reduced, weakened. Secondly, they are mixed up and so it is possible to dream dreams of opposites. Everybody shares the frustration of dreaming of walking over sky or putting on a book instead of a shirt. Such opposites in dreams co-exist because the powers which co-exist in the soul are in a jumbled up state.

So it is with the soul of the world, *Hashem*. When *Hashem*, as it were, is asleep, the level of revelation of G-dliness in the world is weak and is all jumbled up. Bad co-exists with good — not only does it co-exist with good, it seems to totally overtake it. We cannot walk the streets at night without the risk of some head-shaven demented savage trying to attack and kill us.

That night, says the verse, the King woke up; the King was no longer asleep. There was again a revelation of G-dliness. The Jews prayed and fasted for three days and so the King woke up. Esther, one of the most beautiful women in history,[149] was to seek to have King Achashverosh reverse Haman's decree and save the Jewish nation. A natural method would involve the bath house, perfume, the hairdresser and perhaps the lingerie shop. Instead, Esther took the non-natural course of fasting for three days.

Skin goes gray after three days fasting and is accompanied by foul smelling breath. In the moment of her least appeal, Esther is welcomed by the King. This result is outside nature because she was functioning outside nature, the level a Jew can function if he lives as a Jew. With halitosis and gray skin, Esther looked wonderful to Achashverosh and he listened to her. The Jews in the provinces, instead of appointing a committee to lobby and a sub-committee to fundraise, went to synagogue. They fasted for three days and they davened to *Hashem* and were thus able to connect to the inner aspect of G-dliness which is above nature.

This is what we celebrate on Purim. Nature is totally eclipsed and every single Jew is saved.

It is fascinating that, in those moments when there shines holiness revealed by Jews living as Jews, Haman cannot exist. He must die.

This is what Moshiach (the Messianic Redeemer) is. To have Moshiach is to eradicate Haman. There will then be a revelation of G-dliness so strong that it will be impossible for evil to exist. This revelation of G-dliness can only come from Jews living and learning together as Jews.

149. See *Megillas Esther* 2:17 and *Talmud Megillah* 13a.

SECRETS OF THE FESTIVALS
CHAPTER 6

PESACH

On the Tenth of Nissan,[150] four days before Pesach, each Jewish family in *Mitzrayim* (Egypt) took a lamb, tied it to their bedpost, thereby spurning the Egyptian idol worship and readied themselves for the first Pesach sacrifice. The *Midrash* explains that the Egyptians came to the Jews and asked them to explain their actions. The Jews repeated carefully exactly what they were doing without any apologies. They disclosed that in four days there would be a plague in which all the first born would be killed. Understandably, many Egyptians who were first born heard this information with a lack of enthusiasm. They approached Pharaoh, demanding that he listen and let the Jews go, to the point that civil war broke out. We know that many Egyptians died in that civil war and all of that happened on the Tenth of Nissan. In that year, the Tenth was Shabbos; we celebrate it as *Shabbos HaGadol,* the Shabbos before Pesach.

Shabbos HaGadol is about the leaving of *Mitzrayim* (called Egypt but understood as confined, restricted — see Building Block No. 8). It was the merit of their *emunah*[151] which broke down the boundaries encompassing the Jews. *Emunah* is difficult to translate in English; it means, belief, faith, trust, but more than any of those terms, it connotes a form of connection, an interdependence in one's belief.

So at first glance,[152] asks the Rebbe, what has *emunah* to do with escape from restrictions? There can be *emunah* in bondage and

---

150. See *Alter Rebbe's Shulchan Aruch* 430:1.
151. See *Yalkut Shimoni Hoshea, Remez* 519.
152. For the following explanation see *Likkutei Sichos,* Vol. 1, p. 239ff.

there can be *emunah* in escape; one really has nothing to do with the other.

There is an important difference between the nations and Jews in relation to this question of *emunah*. Whereas the nations are regarded in Jewish thought with exactly the same respect as every other facet of creation, there are the differences already discussed. (Building Block No. 6) In addition, a non-Jew and a Jew have an important qualitative difference in their *emunah*.

Non-Jews believe in G-d. However, a non-Jew's belief in G-d is an intellectual accomplishment, a product of reasoning. An intelligent non-Jew observes that everything in the world is created and therefore has a Creator. They make logical connections between the fact that Nature is so staggeringly powerful, deep and wide, that there must be some kind of G-dly-force behind it. This notion is expressed differently. Various religions talk about a Force or a Power. Basically, all express the same thing despite the changes in vocabulary that they recognize that there is a G-d in the world.

This recognition is a product of intellect and reasoning. Nothing however is known about that Force. Reason cannot take the inquiry any further.

The notion of G-dliness is recognized in what can be observed intellectually and in what conclusions can be drawn inescapably from what is observed.

A *neshomah's emunah* does not come from empirical observation; rather, a Jew's *emunah* is there first. A *neshomah* is part of, and so connected to, G-d. The *emunah* in G-d is unshakable and almost irrelevant to observation. In the same way as others are connected to the world, a Jew is connected to *Hashem*. This is the critically important difference and the reason the so-called dialogues between Jews and non-Jews have been such a failure in history. One person is talking Japanese, the other, Chinese. They are both perfectly logical languages in isolation, but there is no point of conjunction. A Jew is expressing an inescapable spiritual condition; a non-Jew is articulating an intellectual and rational position achieved.

Just as a Jew is not limited in the world by his perception of nature, he is not limited in his appreciation of G-dliness.

There are various names for *Hashem*. Here it is sufficient to discuss two. The name *Yud-Hay-Vav-Hay* is used to describe *Hashem* outside of Nature and the name *Elokim* is G-d as concealed in Nature.

The level of *Hashem* described by *Yud-Hay-Vav-Hay* is a description of past, present and future. This is above Nature, as Nature cannot function in terms of the past, present and future all at once. This is outside the scheme of the created existence as time is a created commodity. The name *Elokim* means *Hashem's* concealment by Nature and describes everything created in terms of the physical world. It is logical therefore for people to function within, and be part of, that natural system. It is wrong to ask the remainder of humanity to be anything else as they simply lack the sensory perception.

A Jew, on the other hand, is connected to *Yud-Hay-Vav-Hay*, outside of Nature.

So it was that Pharaoh asks at one point, immediately prior to Israel breaking out of their collective *Mitzrayim*, "Who is this Name *Yud-Hay-Vav-Hay?*" He only knew *Elokim*. It is a common mistake to underestimate the prowess of Pharaoh. He was a man of immense power in *kelipah*, heading up the most powerful nation in the world. But when he said, "I don't know who is this *Yud-Hay-Vav-Hay*", he was telling the truth. He was doing no more or less than making a sincere empirical observation.

Nature comes from *Elokim*, that which is outside Nature (miracles) from *Yud-Hay-Vav-Hay*.

There are two kinds of miracles; miracles which are above and beyond Nature and miracles which are enclothed in Nature. The miracles which are above and beyond Nature are, for example, the Ten Plagues. When you suddenly see hail on fire or water turn to blood, then that is an interference of Nature from outside of Nature. Pharaoh saw and attested to all of those miracles. At the end of all of these, he says, "I don't know who is this Name *Yud-Hay-Vav-Hay*". He sees what is happening above Nature, but it does not compute.

Those miracles which are themselves clothed in Nature are of the kind represented by the phenomenon of Sadam Hussein's scud missiles. We all lived through this recently. We learned that forty-one missiles over a short period of time were discharged over *Eretz Yisrael* and not one person in Israel died directly from a hit. The most hardened, non-observant Jew freely recognized this as a miracle. Within a month or two of the events, the world, led by the Press, agreed that the rockets were deficient, there was inadequate technology, the Russians sabotaged them — any reason that could be found was found providing that reason could be reduced to natural terms.

To this day, the world has forgotten that it really was a miracle; they chose to remember that there was something wrong with the machines. After all they were required to be buried under the sand. Maybe all the reasoned reasons play a part. There is a need among non-Jews to relate their experiences to, and support them by, Nature. There is a need in a Jew however to look totally outside of Nature and to relate their experiences to their direct connection with *Hashem*. In fact, says the Rebbe, in a Jew the position is reversed. A Jew will come to a conclusion that first it is G-d only, then there is Nature.

The *Talmud Yerushalmi* says "a Jew prays to *Hashem* and them sows his grain." Why? he knows as a farmer that the ground will grow the grain in accordance with Nature. He knows that the exigencies of storms, pestilence or famine are the prerogative of *Hashem*. So his first point of reference is *Hashem*. Has he behaved according to law, has he been good to his mother, did he talk *Loshon Hora* (defamingly)? Satisfied with his calculation, only then does he know its produce. This is the psyche of the Jewish nation.

The splitting of the Red Sea (as it mistranslated) is another example of an event unanimously accepted as a miracle by the Jewish nation. Not only is the story told in the *Chumash* (the Written Torah) but the details are punctiliously explained in the oral law later transcribed to the Talmud and the *Midrash*. The miracle was so obvious, explains the *Midrash*, that when the sea divided, all water that had been collected in one place, anywhere in the world, also divided.

It is interesting that nearly all geophysical accounts of the splitting of the Red Sea are by non-Jews. Consistently, any version always tracks along a natural explanation. It was the east wind, it was the fact that the Nile (!) dries up at that time; any possible convolution which may yield a rational explanation. Some say it never happened at all. Leaving aside such fraud, those non-Jews who seriously try and come to terms with the fact that it happened will accept it at a rational level, forcing the facts to fit into preconceived natural patterns.

The reason that Jews were afforded the opportunity to be released from *Mitzrayim* (bondage) was because of their *emunah*. It was because they, prior to Matan Torah, were connected by their choice to *Hashem* and of course that connection was outside of and beyond Nature.

Redemption from limitations exists at two distinct levels. There is a level in *kelipah*, badness, where a person can be so limited and so immersed in the *kelipah* around him that he can almost forget *Hashem*, so descending to what is called the 49th level of Impurity, a pitifully low and miserable state. This was the point to which Israel had sunk prior to their escape from *Mitzrayim*.

There is however, a level of limitation in *kedushah* (holiness) where a Jew can be in *Mitzrayim*, not only some 3,500 years ago but immediately before Pesach in every year and indeed every day. His appreciation of G-dliness becomes limited; his awareness of his connection to *Hashem* as being outside of nature becomes muddied and limited by the natural environment. To this Jew, his environment seems to define him in the same way as it does a non-Jew. The progress through life and the solving of the trials and problems that a Jewish *neshomah* has to solve are seen as part of the natural fabric. This is real *Mitzrayim*. For a Jewish *neshomah*, this is total jail. What is the key to escape? Only the merit of *emunah*.

This is the secret of Pesach, prefaced by *Shabbos HaGadol*. This is the secret of the eight days of Pesach and, in particular, the two *sedarim.* The process of escape is no longer a physical process, our *neshomos* have done that in the past. It is the recurring process of escaping that reinforced goal of spiritual limitation which is the secret of Pesach. A Jewish *neshomah* must not be oppressed and goaled by its host nation in its perspective. Unless that perspective can be changed to that of a Jew outside of the constraints of his physical environment, Jewish life is wasted.

This level is difficult to attain every day when dealing with the business thieves of everyday life. Certainly, the accomplishment is greater every generation when the tests for the *neshomah's* in every *gilgul* increase in difficulty.

The merit of their *emunah* which did not reckon with Nature is the same merit that takes a Jew out of his *Mitzrayim* on Pesach and on a daily basis.

Not being concerned about looking different, having a beard, wearing a *yarmulke* and wearing *tzitzis* is the way out. The greatest bondage for a Jew is to imagine his welfare as being dependent on the non-Jewish view of him. The greatest escape comes from not being aware of their outlook but being totally conscious of only our connection to and dependence upon *Hashem.*

This is why we eat *matzah* on Pesach. *Matzah* is called the bread of *emunah*[153] and accordingly symbolizes our connection to *Hashem. Chometz* (leaven) and *matzah* in Hebrew share the same letters, but reversed. *Chometz* connotes being puffed up and bloated and full of one's self-importance.[154] *Emunah* cannot co-exist with *yeshus* (feeling of a persons self-importance) (See Building Block No. 4). When a person is blown up with his own self-importance, there is no room left for *emunah* in *Hashem.* The state of *emunah* is a contrary state of *yeshus.* The more *yeshus,* the less *emunah.*

One of the secrets of Torah is that the way to reach the requisite level of *emunah* is to get rid of the *chometz.* Clean it out of the houses, cars, pockets and our system altogether. Then, when instead we eat *matzah* which has no leaven. This *matzah* has to be

---

153. See *HaYom Yom,* Entry 15 Nissan.
154. See *Likkutei Torah, Leviticus* 13ff.

scrupulously chosen *matzah*. The *matzah*, free of leaven, affords the opportunity of and space for *emunah*. By eating it, we take in the power to re-focus our *emunah* for the coming year so equipping us with the keys to break forth from spiritual bondage and limitation.

SECRETS OF THE FESTIVALS
CHAPTER 7

LAG B'OMER

Lag B'Omer is a *Yom Tov* which is not from the Torah but from the Rabbis. Lag B'Omer is the *Yartzeit* of R. Shimon Bar Yochai, the author of the *Zohar,* mentioned previously.[155]

In Eretz Yisrael, Lag B'Omer is celebrated with great enthusiasm.

On one of our trips to Israel, we hired a Torah-observant Guide. He was an extraordinary man whose daily routine was to rise at 2:00 am and learn and pray until 10:00 am. From 10:00 am he would work for however much time he needed to accumulate enough to pay rent, food, clothing, school fees and the Shabbos needs. If he had accumulated this amount, he would stop work for the week and spend the remaining days learning.

Our Guide took us to Miron in the foothills outside Tzfat where R. Shimon Bar Yochai is buried. It is a long drive from Jerusalem where we stayed, to Miron. The Guide did not drive. His system was to hire a taxi and then deliver to the passengers, willing or not, a *shiur* in Torah for the duration of the journey. Any attempts to interrupt to ask questions about the passing landscape were put down with rigid authority.

He told us that in 1948, when Israel was still occupied by British soldiers, a woman had brought her very sick child to Miron to the tomb where R. Shimon Bar Yochai and his son are buried one beside the other. Being a place where wonders take place, many of the sick and the poor congregate in Miron on Lag B'Omer in the hope of miraculous intervention.

---

155. See *Pri Eitz Chaim, Shaar* 22 Chapter 6.

Our Guide solemnly attested that, according to the British army personnel, the child died. The hysterical mother placed the child on the grave of R. Shimon Bar Yochai and, to the bewilderment of the Anglo-Saxon army staff, began shrieking at the stone.

Apparently, after being barren for eleven years, she received a blessing for a child on Lag B'Omer when she was previously at Miron. Now she screamed to the stone that she was not leaving until either she died or the child was resuscitated. Any attempt to move her by the distraught soldiers would have been a life risk.

Suddenly, to the shivering spines of the witnesses, the child emitted a low cry. The woman, after slowly composing herself, gathered up her child and walked through the throng of gaping observers. The child has now grown to be a significant scholar learning in the *Yeshivah* of our Guide. We arrived having sniffed a breath of the atmosphere of Miron and the mists of wonders that swirl around Lag B'Omer.

Rabbi Akiva was a shepherd,[156] who at the age of forty could not read the *Alef-Beis*. He subsequently developed into one of the greatest scholars in the history of Jewish learning. The story goes that he was once watching a stone notched by the steady dripping of water. He concluded that if water could penetrate stone, Torah could penetrate his head. His employer's daughter heard of his resolve and was so touched by his sincerity to learn that she married him. She encouraged him to go away to learn Torah in a *Yeshivah* where he remained for twelve years. After his return from the academy, his wife once again agreed that he should again go away to learn. He reappeared a second time with twenty four thousand *talmidim* (students). When she tried to get near to greet him, his wife was held back.

R. Akiva intervened and publicly told his students that all his Torah, and all the twenty four thousand students belonged to her. From this we learn the rule that the Torah learned by a husband

---

156. See *Kesubos* 62b.

with the permission of his wife is equally credited to the merit of the wife.[157]

Of the twenty four thousand students, all but five died progressively between Pesach and Shavuos.[158] It is one of the great tragedies in the history of Jewish learning that they died in such epidemic proportion, so quickly and in so specific a time. The most distinguished of the students left alive was R. Shimon Bar Yochai, buried at Miron.

R. Shimon Bar Yochai is synonymous with *Kabbalah*. As mentioned earlier, he wrote the *Zohar,* its fundamental text, generally unavailable to Jews for one thousand years.

The content of that book forms a basis of *Chassidus* in general and *Chabad Chassidus* in particular.

The astonishing life and the influence of R. Shimon Bar Yochai is impossible to exaggerate. Escaping from the Romans[159] who had just killed R. Akiva, he and his son hid in a cave for thirteen years. The ground of this cave was made of deep dried sand. The *Tzaddikim* dug two holes. During the day they lived in the holes, covered to their necks in sand in order to study Torah. When they prayed they emerged and dressed. At the mouth of the cave was a carob tree and a stream of fresh water which sustained them throughout their ordeal.

Lag B'Omer celebrates two connected things. The first is the conclusion of the dying of the students of R. Akiva on Lag B'Omer leaving only five students alive. The second is that it is the date on which R. Shimon Bar Yochai himself subsequently died.

There are very significant differences between the deaths of these two giants. R. Akiva died a martyr's death. It had been ordered by the Romans that no Torah was to be learned in public. R. Akiva ignored this edict and, when detected, was tortured to death by the Romans, combed with combs of red hot metal. He died, although in horrible pain, in a state of ecstasy having fulfilled all the *mitzvos*

---

157. See *Berachos* 17a.
158. See *Yevamos* 62b.
159. See *Shabbos* 33b.

including that of dying a martyr's death to glorify the Name of G-d.[160] R. Shimon Bar Yochai, on the other hand, died quietly and requested prior to his death that on his *Yartzeit*, the Jewish world should rejoice greatly.

When a *Tzaddik* dies, his life purpose of learning Torah and doing *mitzvos* is realized, bringing him to a state of perfection.[161]

Children learn that the twenty four thousand *talmidim* of R. Akiva, on the other hand, died because of lack of mutual respect which eclipsed their greatness in learning. Children learn that, because *Hashem* was displeased with the service of the *talmidim*, they died.

Consider this however; we are talking of twenty four thousand scholars, the lowest in learning of whom was very learned in his own right. These men who had spent up to twenty years with R. Akiva, often separated from their wives and children, were absorbed in building a spiritual ladder to G-d and devoting their whole existence to the precipitation of Moshiach.

Yet this army of Torah giants are put to death because they had no mutual respect! How can this be? Since, as we have seen, the fundamental teaching of R. Akiva was to love your fellow Jew as yourself,[162] we can be sure that the twenty four thousand *talmidim* knew this notion well. How can it be therefore that they did not have any respect for each other?

A dog can be taught to walk to heel by repeating the instruction over and over again until the dog understands it. There are however two ways of repeating the instruction. One person functioning at the level of *chesed* (kindness), whenever the dog walks to heel, will fall all over the dog, pat it, praise it and reward it. The dog learns through positive reinforcement. The other, functioning at the level of *gevurah* (strength or strictness), will kick and punish the dog whenever it does not walk to heel. This dog will learn in order to avoid being punished. Both methods are legitimate routes to the same achievement.

---

160. Mentioned in the *Mussaf Prayers* of *Yom Kippur*.
161. See *Tanya, Iggeres HaKodesh* Epistle 27.
162. See *Sifra on Leviticus* 19:18.

As R. Akiva taught his students, each converted the knowledge
to their own personal mental set. Each valuing so greatly his
teaching and each being of such a lofty level they could not tolerate
any different approach. One man heard R. Akiva teaching Chesed,
another heard *gevurah*. Each then believed the other to be missing
something and so each man's mission became the endeavor to
convince the other of his lack, and vice versa.[163]

There is a notion in *Chassidus* of *mashpia* (giver) and *mekabel*
(receiver). *Mashpia* refers to the one giving over and *mekabel*
means the one receiving. A physical manifestation of this spiritual
notion is man and woman. When man and woman procreate, man
is the *mashpia* and woman is the *mekabel*. This process exists
throughout creation. In education, the teacher is *mashpia*, the
student the *mekabel*. For the current of life to flow, both must be
there; without one, there is sterility.

Everyone of R. Akiva's Chassidim was a *mashpia* and nobody a
mekabel. None had an interest in listening to each other. All
believed they had listened to R. Akiva. Each insisted on their own
way and each meant well; but life's fulfillment requires a man to be
a *mekabel* as well as a *mashpia*.

Additionally, the students suffered a further and deeper
disability.[164] It is an important secret of Torah to return to the
physical after rising to the spiritual. As we shall see, R. Akiva had
perfected this.

Four *Tzaddikim* entered *Pardes* (heaven) and gazed upon all the
secrets of Torah. Three of them were harmed, only R. Akiva
returned in peace.[165] Why? Three of them were able to rise but not
return. R. Akiva climbed with a view that the rise would be followed
by a return. He would return and bring back what he experienced
there to benefit the world at its physical level.

A flight to *Hashem* without a return to the physical is of no use.
Mankind are not intended to be angels. Angels fly spiritually,
constantly. Animals look only to eat, drink and escape every

163. For this explanation see *Likkutei Sichos,* Vol. 22, p. 139.
164. See *Ibid.*
165. See *Chagigah* 14b.

inconvenience. The greatness of humanity in general, and *neshomos* in particular, is our obligation for both flight and food. We must penetrate heaven but bring that information back to the mundane physical to make a dwelling place for G-d on Earth. To simply climb into heaven and stay there is to abandon our responsibility to the physical. For that there is no reason for a *neshomah* to descend into a body. It could always have remained in its spiritual plane.

That was the punishment of the students of R. Akiva. Each man, a *mashpia*, wanted to rise alone to drink the nectars of the secrets of the universe. To be a *mekabel*, grounding the learning in physicality eluded them!

All the greatness of being a *talmid* of R. Akiva was thus nullified and led only to death.

R. Shimon Bar Yochai survived because of his devotion to the return. No matter what dizzying heights he and his son scaled from their holes in the sand, they brought back the treasures of those visions and translated them into practical service, both for themselves and for all Israel.

This is what we celebrate in joy on Lag B'Omer; the fruits of his perceptions are dug back into the ground of practical observance. The physical is infused with the spiritual.

The fruits of those visions still wave gently in the breezes of Miron.

SECRETS OF THE FESTIVALS
CHAPTER 8

SHAVUOS

Shavuos takes place fifty days after Pesach. We count the Omer for 49 days from Pesach to Shavuos. Pesach as we have learned is the notion of escaping bondage and breaking personal boundaries.

Shavuos is the celebration of the time at which the Torah was given to the Jewish nation on Mount Sinai.[166] This was a unique moment in time, the only occasion on which there has been a revelation of G-dliness to a vast group of people. There have been many individuals who claim to have had sensory contact with the Almighty. Perhaps they have. Clearly there is always room in such cases for skepticism.

At that moment in history three million people experienced something beyond comparison which has been carefully recorded and reproduced from generation to generation from the time of the giving of the Torah. In fact we have an uninterrupted chain of testimony commencing from the three million people who experienced this incident. Moshe took six hundred thousand males together with their women and children out of Egypt, into the desert, out of bondage, breaking all boundaries to do so. Forty-eight days later, he was told to prepare everybody for the fact that *Hashem* was going to appear. Three days before the Torah was given, the forty-eighth day, the Jews prepared themselves for what was to be one of the most cataclysmic events in human history.

On the sixth of Sivan, amidst thunder, lightning and every imaginable backdrop all three million people heard the Ten

---

166. See *Alter Rebbe's Shulchan Aruch* 494:1.

Commandments.[167] These same Ten Commandments are read in synagogue every Shavuos.

What happened the day the Torah was given changed the effect of human behavior for all time.

Prior to the giving of the Torah, that which was spiritual was spiritual and that which was physical remained physical; there was no conjunction between the two. Now, for the first time since creation, mankind was able to bring down into physicality that which was spiritual.[168]

A shattering corollary can be deduced from this astonishing fact; not only can objects be infused with the spiritual but the spiritual can actually be effected by what is done in the physical. *Neshomos* can literally change the course of what is to happen according to the way in which they respond to the *mitzvos*. For the first time in history *Hashem* commanded a nation to keep six hundred and thirteen *mitzvos* and learn His newly revealed Torah. The astonishing result is that the behavior of the *neshomos* orchestrates the present and the future of everything alive on the globe.[169]

Accordingly when a Jew puts on *tefillin*, the mere act of putting on that *tefillin* effects spiritual change. The Rebbe in many of his letters repeatedly points out that a man can improve the *berachos* (blessings) which flow to him by his actions.[170] These of course relate to performing *mitzvos*. These physical activities of the Jew at a personal level effect a change for him as well as generally in the spiritual dimension.

If a Jew eats kosher for example, eating a cow which eats the grass which is grown by the ground; the cow, the grass and the ground are elevated by the Jew using that food to nourish his body to learn Torah and do *mitzvos*.[171] Physical activity effects a spiritual

167. See *Exodos* 19:16, 20:15.
168. See for example *Likkutei Sichos*, Vol. 1, p. 40ff.
169. See for example *Sefer HaMaamarim Melukot* Vol. 1, p. 14 in explanation of the *Midrash* "Know what is above you".
170. See for example *Igros Kodesh of the Rebbe*, Vol. 7, p. 180.
171. See *Igros Melech* Vol. 1, p. 320.

result. So it is generally that *neshomos* cause a change in physicality which effects spirituality which fascinatingly enough then can change physicality again.

Indeed, when Israel behaves in accordance with Torah and *mitzvos* we have peace and plenty in the world. History can be studied as a reflection of Jewish activity; in times of Jewish integrity the world moves forward in harmony. When Jews behave badly the world suffers.

What are the dynamics of this? There are 248 limbs and 365 sinews in the human body (see Building Block no. 5). Just as they need exercise and blood to sustain and keep them healthy so the limbs and sinews of the world are sustained by the exercise of *mitzvos* and the life blood of Torah. By our learning the Torah and keeping the *mitzvos* we draw down G-dliness into the physical so sustaining the world.

It is this very power to bring down the spiritual and infuse the physical which from then on became the mission of the Jewish nation. The ultimate achievement will be to fulfill G-d's purpose in creating the physical world. That purpose as set out previously, is to make a dwelling place for Him in the lowest of all worlds — the physical.[172]

This awesome power was given to us at Mt. Sinai and this is what we celebrate on Shavuos. When finally the job is complete, when all physicality has been soaked to saturation with G-dliness, Moshiach will be revealed. Then G-dliness will be as evident and revealed as sunshine and warmth are today and Israel will have completed *Hashem's* intent for Creation.

There is a second aspect to our celebration of the giving of the Torah. This second aspect somehow escapes most people. Even when Jews learn Torah in depth there seems to be a problem converting the principle we will now discuss into *daas* (see Building Block no. 3). This is so even though many have read and heard the precept. Let us begin with the simple proposition; the Torah, being the wisdom of *Hashem* and His truth, is eternal.

---

172. See *Tanya*, Chapter 33.

Doesn't sound too difficult? The Torah applies in each generation, to every Jew, every day. Obviously, at its simple level this means there can be no change in our everyday laws of Shabbos, *Kashrus* and all those matters which legally separate us from the rest of society.

At a deeper level the concept is much more exciting. Just as the Torah applies in general to every Jew, each week's *Sedra* (portion) applies specially in that week. Indeed each days portion applies to that day![173]

So for example, when we learn the day's Torah portion telling of the binding of Isaac by Abraham, the opportunity for the spiritual potential is there for each Jew on that day to achieve a level of self sacrifice. This can be at a spiritual or physical level.

Deeper still, equipped with this secret, when a Jew learns that *Hashem* appeared to Abraham he can check what Abraham was doing to merit the revelation. He can then be certain that, because of this principle that the Torah is eternal and applicable to every Jew, he could invoke the same revelation as Abraham — providing he satisfied the same conditions.[174] Again, this will be easiest in the week of the relevant portion. Suddenly therefore every Jew has a map! Everyday is charted by Torah at a level of potential. Tuning in to the plan allows for sense to be made from confusion, music to be separated from static.

As mentioned repeatedly *daas* in these concepts requires personal achievement rather than outside instruction. However, when a Jew learns there is treasure at home, he can at least make the decision of whether to dig for it.

On Shavuos those who have been digging, (and finding, as every Jewish excavator does), come together to celebrate the fact that we were given life's precious blueprint and exalt in its contents — each man at his level.

---

173. See *HaYom Yom,* Entry 2, 3 Cheshvan.
174. See *Likkutei Sichos,* Vol. 1, p. 23ff.

EPILOGUE

WHY DO BAD THINGS HAPPEN TO GOOD PEOPLE?

If this book has been written properly, this Epilogue should not be necessary. For the sake of completeness however we learn it together.

We begin with a reminder of the concept of *Hashgochah Protis* (Divine Providence) (see Building Block No. 1). All of creation is constantly being brought into existence by *Hashem's* effortless concentration and this entails control of every atom and molecule all the time. The only rider on this as we have seen is the area of free choice in relation to moral decisions — 613 areas for Jews, 7 for non-Jews.

The second reminder is that G-d is all good (see Building Block No. 2).

So the reader has surely gleaned the reality already. It follows that if there is total *Hashgochah Protis* over everything and if *Hashem* is all good, there can be no bad. There is our *perception* of bad but a moment's thought will allow everybody to understand, given the first two principles, that bad itself must be purposeful and for the good.

So let us take an example. Let us pretend that there is a trip for two to the Paris available as a prize. In order to secure the prize one must learn a basic level of French. This level, let us further pretend, is assessed by examination. This examination is to have four separate parts and there are four books available for study, one for each part. For the purpose of this example, we pretend you want the prize and we will analyze the steps as follows:

1. Book No. 3 is out of print and is
    therefore unavailable.   BAD

2. You learn remaining three books and attend
   the exam. No questions on book No. 3!   GOOD

3. Book No. 3 is out of print and is
   therefore unavailable.   NOW GOOD

4. You pass the exam and win the prize.   GOOD

5. Plane leaves the next day. You have
   seemingly insufficient time to pack.   BAD

6. You have packed after all. Plane leaves
   the next day. You have seemingly
   insufficient time to pack.   NOW GOOD

7. Taxi to the airport has an accident
   delaying you.   BAD

8. You miss plane.   BAD

9. Plane crashes killing everyone on board.

10. Taxi to the airport has an accident
    delaying you.   NOW GOOD

11. You miss plane.   NOW GOOD

Can you see what is happening? We keep having to rewrite what is good or bad as more information comes in. The third book not being available is bad without the extra information that it is not required; then its unavailability becomes a good. Winning the prize seems good until the fatal flight and then is a bad. The taxi accident is bad until the plane crash and then becomes a good. Missing the plane at first bad becomes a good. Careful thought brings this; IT DEPENDS AT WHAT POINT OF TIME YOU VIEW THE EVIDENCE. Without subsequent evidence, no decision can be made.

There is a Law in Torah that that which comes from kosher is kosher. There can be no bad coming from *Hashem* because *Hashem* is all good. It follows that all that comes from Him must be good.

What about those things apparently bad? It cannot be denied that there is apparent bad everywhere. Natural disasters, sickness, pain and suffering, death. These are realities and cannot be denied.

As we have learned, there are three areas of *berochas* (see Building Block No. 2). Some people are given all three, some two and some people, none. There have been great *Tzaddikim* with none and they have been very happy and they did not view their lives as miserable. Why? The answer is that they recognize a reality; that every human being is tested day in and day out in this world. Furthermore, the purpose of these tests is for the good. A *Tzaddik* will recognize that every *yeridah* is for the sake of an *aliyah* (see Building Block No. 2). As we have seen, a person can either try to grow from that situation, try to tune into the spiritual forces which are giving him the opportunity of that apparently negative test; or he can become despondent and view the test as bad. To do so is as short-sighted as being despondent at the taxi breaking down. Until all the evidence is in, a man cannot know. He only sees a few pages of the book and it is the pages he has not yet seen which will determine his judgment.

If then everything is for the good and tests are beneficial, why do we not beat our breasts and beg *Hashem* to test us? Why do we constantly ask for things which seem to us to be good? If, as has been implied, there is no difference, why be concerned at being barren, poor or sick? The answer is that it is human to want that which appears good to us to the exclusion of that which we do not perceive as good for us. We do not want to be tested; we beg *Hashem* not to test us. But if tested, it is critical to grasp that ultimately the test is only for good. It is entirely natural however to ask *Hashem* for experiences that not only are for our good but which we can perceive as good.

There remains however a problem; we learn in *Chassidus* that there are four worlds: *Atzilus, Beriah, Yetzirah* and our world, *Asiyah*. We learn that in *Atzilus*, there is no bad; in *Beriah*, bad is separated off; in *Yetzirah*, bad and good exist in equal proportions and in *Asiyah*, bad is predominant over good. Empirical evidence is that in our world there is more bad than good. So how do the two notions stand together? On the one hand, we say there is no bad; on the other, we say that we live in a world in which there is more bad than good. Deeper, we know that the charge of *neshomos Yisrael* is to be moved around the globe from country to country elevating their collective *Nefesh HaBahamis* and refining and purifying the good from the bad. How then can it be said there is no bad?

There are two categories of bad. There is first the perceived bad of a test. This we know now not to be bad but an opportunity for development. The other aspect of bad is *kelipah* (opposite to holiness). *kelipah* means a husk, shell. The shell, the *kelipah* is responsible for a lack of revelation of G-dliness. When we talk of elevating the bad, we refer to a Jewish *neshomah* taking something that is *kelipah* and bringing a revelation of G-dliness to it through physical activity. This is fundamentally different to a test. Here, there is an absence of revealed G-dliness where our task is to convert darkness into light. This is, after all, our mission on earth for the time the *neshomah* is in the body.

So really there is no bad at all. There are various goods; those which come in terms of tests which require practice to identify as such. Separately, there are those things with which a Jew comes into contact, where there exists an opportunity to elevate and refine. Our task is to reveal the apparent lack of G-dliness, so bringing good.

What of children who die, people with terrible terminal diseases, great natural disasters or deliberate human evil? A Jew's heart must break with pity and empathy. One of our most important tests is to help. Every action is worth a thousand sighs. But the truth is that ultimately it cannot be said not to be good until all the evidence is in; and the evidence is not in in one lifetime and it is not in in one consciousness. That we know as Torah.

So at this Epilogue together we have now some of the equipment with which to live. We have the *chochmah* and *binah* that everything is Divinely controlled and for good; we have the *chochmah* and *binah* that being a Jew is fundamentally purposeful. We have the *chochmah* and *binah* that to tune into that purpose allows us to build a dwelling place for *Hashem* in the physical world — the whole reason for creation. And we have the *chochmah* and *binah* to do all this with joy. As a by-product, true happiness will result.

All that is *chochmah* and *binah*. The *daas*, as has been said before, must come from the reader. Torah warms the hands and feet. It requires effort and practice to exclude everything else from the mind and heart. To do so turns the darkest night into blazing daylight.

LIST OF THE LUBAVITCHER *REBBEIM*

1. "THE ALTER REBBE", RABBI SHNEUR ZALMAN.
    Born 5505 (1745). So great was his learning that at 13 he was accepted as equal to scholars of the previous generation. Definer of *Chabad Chassidus*. Author of the Cornerstone of *Chabad Chassidus,* the *Tanya.*
    Passed away 5583 (1812).

2. "THE MITTELER REBBE" RABBI DOVBER.
    Born 5534 (1773) son of the Alter Rebbe, author of an abundance of volumes of *Chassidus*, and founder of *Chabad* settlements.
    Passed away 5588 (1827).

3. "THE TZEMACH TZEDEK" RABBI MENACHEM MENDEL.
    Born 5549 (1789) Grandson of the Alter Rebbe, prodigious genius, compiler of his grandfather's Torah as well as prolific expounder of Torah in his own right. Honored in Secular politics as well as leading *Chabad.* Author of much *Chassidus*.
    Passed away 5626 (1866).

4. "THE REBBE MAHARASH" RABBI SHMUEL.
    Born 5594 (1834). Successful in nullifying many decrees and pogroms against the Jews. Author of much *Chassidus*.
    Passed Away 5643 (1882).

5. "THE REBBE RASHAB" RABBI SHOLOM DOVBER.
    Born 5621 (1860). Established Lubavitcher Yeshivahs, lobbied successfully for Jewish affairs and authored many of the most studied texts of *Chassidus*.
    Passed away 5680 (1920) leaving one son.

6.   "THE PREVIOUS REBBE" RABBI YOSEF YITZCHAK.
       Born 5640 (1880) moved permanently to N.Y. in 1940
       moving much of modern observant Jewry to the USA.
       Sender of Emissaries spreading *Chabad*. Author of a wide
       scope of *Chassidus* from the most complex to that brought
       down to the most comprehensible levels as yet in history.
       Passed away 5710 (1950).

7.   "THE REBBE" RABBI MENACHEM MENDEL SCHNEERSON.
       Born 5662 (1902) seventh leader of Lubavitcher Chassidim.
       Torah genius, Scientist, Prophet, leader of and example to
       our generation.
       Passed away 5754 (1994).